SUSTAINING THE FUTURE
OF OUR PLANET
TOGETHER

SUSTAINING THE FUTURE OF OUR PLANET

The Prophetic Ministry of Pope Francis and Ecumenical Patriarch Bartholomew

Edited by John Chryssavgis and Angela Caliaro

HOLY CROSS
ORTHODOX PRESS
Brookline, Massachusettes

@ 2024 John Chryssavgis and Angela Caliaro
All rights reserved. Except for brief quotations in critical publications or reviews, no part of this book may be reproduced in any form without permission of the publisher.
Cover Photo, Courtesy of the Archons of the Ecumenical Patriarchate

Published by
Holy Cross Orthodox Press
Hellenic College, Inc.
50 Goddard Avenue, Brookline, MA 02445

ISBN: 978-1-9660613-04-2
Publishers Cataloging-in-Publication
(Provided by Cassidy Cataloguing Services, Inc.)

Names: Chryssavgis, John, editor. | Caliaro, Angela, editor.
Title: Sustaining the future of our planet together : the prophetic ministry of Pope Francis and Ecumenical Patriarch Bartholomew / edited by John Chryssavgis and Angela Caliaro.
Description: Brookline, Massachusetts : Holy Cross Orthodox Press, [2024].
Identifiers: ISBN: 978-1-960613-04-2
Subjects: LCSH: Francis, Pope, 1936- --Political and social views. | Bartholomew I, Ecumenical Patriarch of Constantinople, 1940- --Political and social views. | Ecotheology. | Environmentalism--Religious aspects--Christianity. | Environmental responsibility-- Religious aspects--Christianity. | Environmental protection--Religious aspects--Christianity. | Human ecology--Religious aspects--Christianity. | Social ethics--Religious aspects-- Christianity. | Theology--Environmental aspects. | Orthodox Eastern Church--Theology. | Catholic Church--Theology.
Classification: LCC: BT695.5 .S87 2024 | DDC: 261.88--dc23

CONTENTS

I. INTRODUCTION

Foreword
    John Chryssavgis and Angela Caliaro   xi

Opening Remarks
    Margaret Karram   xvii

Keynote Address
    Ecumenical Patriarch Bartholomew   xxi

II. THEOLOGICAL PERSPECTIVES

1. The Trinity in Creation
    Piero Coda   3

2. Eco-Dogmatics and Eco-Praxis
    Nikolaos Asproulis   19

3. Eco-Theology and Spirituality
    Augoustinos Bairactaris   35

4. Evangelical and Educational Perspectives
    Vincenzo Zani   69

III. ETHICAL, LEGAL, AND ECUMENICAL PERSPECTIVES

5. Ecological Sin
    Chris Durante   85

6. Environmental Law
    Vincenzo Buonomo   123

7. The Holy See and the Ecumenical Patriarchate
    Sandra Ferreira Ribeiro   153

IV. SOCIAL PERSPECTIVES

8. Ecology and Social Doctrine: *Fratelli Tutti*
   Giuseppe Argiolas — 171
9. Social Perspectives: Orthodox and Catholic
   Vasilios Makrides — 183
10. The Roots of a Crisis
    Sergio Rondinara — 225

V. CONCLUSION

11. Addressing the Ecological Crisis Together
    Metropolitan Job — 241

    Final Statement — 255

    Biographical Notes — 257

ABBREVIATIONS

CEC	Conference of European Churches
EG	*Evangelii Gaudium*
FLOW	*For the Life of the World*
FT	*Fratelli Tutti*
ITC	International Theological Commission
LS	*Laudato Si'*
WCC	World Council of Churches

I. INTRODUCTION

FOREWORD

John Chryssavgis and Angela Caliaro

It is a very special privilege to welcome all of you on behalf of His All-Holiness Ecumenical Patriarch Bartholomew to the Fifth Halki Summit, our first gathering after the period of the COVID-19 worldwide pandemic. With the grace of God, we are able to be here in person, to connect with one another and to address vital issues that affect our communities, our churches, and our world. Our esteemed and beloved cosponsor for this summit is the Sophia University Institute.

This particular summit is unique inasmuch as it brings together (at least primarily) Orthodox and Catholics to reflect on the ecological inspiration and initiatives of our respective global religious leaders, Ecumenical Patriarch Bartholomew and Pope Francis. Not only are we blessed that these two bishops share a close relationship with one another, but we are also fortunate that they share the same concerns and the same goals for their congregations. Above all, both of them share the conviction that the followers of Christ must be in communion with one another and that they must together face the challenges of our time.

To this end, from the very beginning of Pope Francis' ministry, when Patriarch Bartholomew attended his installation mass in Rome, they have visited one another in Rome and Constantinople, they have jointly visited places such as Jerusalem (to commemorate the visit to the Holy Land by their predecessors Athenagoras and Paul VI), Lesvos (to bring attention to suffering refugees), and Cairo (to advocate against religious persecution and for religious freedom). In addition, they have issued joint statements on protection of the environment and for peace in the world.

There are many reasons for us to recall and observe this close friendship between our spiritual leaders. In fact, just a few days ago, our Roman Catholic brothers and sisters commemorated the Feast of Pentecost, highlighting the descent of the Holy Spirit that realizes the presence of God in all creation. Moreover, over the next few days, we are celebrating the name-day of His All-Holiness, when we will commemorate his patron Saint, the apostle Bartholomew. They say that green is the color of God's divine Spirit; and of course green is the title that the Ecumenical Patriarch has earned with his environmental leadership.

Nevertheless, this summit is not only a manifestation of our Patriarch's fraternal collaboration with Pope Francis. It is also a reflection of the way His All-Holiness has understood how we must address the ecological crisis from the very outset of his ministry. In raising awareness about climate change, while above all proclaiming the need for us to change our attitudes and actions toward the rest of God's creation, he has always stressed the importance for our approach to be collaborative, collective, and communal. This is why he emphasizes that the environmental initiatives of the Ecumenical Patriarchate—its symposia, summits and seminars—must be inter-religious and inter-disciplinary. We are, after all, all in this *together*! As His All-Holiness has observed, we share a common responsibility for our future; only together can we adequately respond to the ecological crisis. Our vocation as Christians is to establish and enhance connections that can transform the world. In that respect, this summit is a laboratory where we can create these connections.

This meeting is precisely a tribute to the Patriarch's vision, conviction, and commitment. Just look at those who are gathered here this evening, those who have dedicated their time and love to travel to the Phanar and to Halki to deliberate on the subject dearest to the heart of His All-Holiness over the last thirty years and more. They have come from literally every discipline, background, and nation (representing the United States of America, Western

Europe, Great Britain, and the Middle East, as well as Africa, Asia, and South America). As speakers and participants, moderators and organizers, they include:

- Clergy and laity
- Monks and nuns
- Men and women
- Teachers and students
- Authors, editors, and interpreters
- Administrators and consultants
- Political economists and political scientists
- Business specialists and bioethicists
- Theologians and philosophers
- Educationalists and ecumenists
- Legal scholars and canon lawyers
- Ecologists and scientists
- Environmental, chemical, and industrial engineers
- Musicians and composers
- Physicists, dentists, and pharmacists
- Sociologists and social anthropologists
- Policy advisors and landscape architects
- Classicists, orientalists, and islamicists
- Psychologists and neuropsychologists

The presence here of speakers and participants from the most diverse backgrounds and with such varied interdisciplinary and ecumenical experiences will serve as occasions of enrichment but also of communion—of mutual, free, and open conversation and exchange. We know that we live at a decisive turning point for the future of humanity and our planet. So, as we talk about creation care and the desire for unity among our sister churches, each of us has a unique opportunity to learn and grow.

This means that, what our Patriarch has dreamed of and worked for throughout his ministry, is materialized before our eyes. We are all here to learn from what he and his brother Francis have inspired and taught us. And we all are here in common, all here in conversation, all here *together*. Allow me to remind everyone that the English term "conversation" implies "leaning in toward one another" in order to pay close attention, in order to listen carefully. Just as the Greek equivalent for conversation "συζήτησις" implies that we are together on a search for the same goal: to reflect on the ecological inspiration and initiatives of our respective global religious leaders.

OPENING REMARKS

Margaret Karram

It is a great honor and a privilege to bring the greetings of the whole Focolare movement to this fifth edition of the Halki Summits in which we look at the prophetic ministry of Pope Francis and Ecumenical Patriarch Bartholomew towards the future of our common home. The environmental crisis is indeed one of the most urgent and critical issues of the world today. It's high time to think together, to pray together, and to act together to sustain the future of our planet.

The ecumenical patriarchate of Constantinople has played a formidable leading role in this context. For over three decades, His All-Holiness Patriarch Bartholomew has shown great leadership in affirming the profound theological and spiritual roots underlying his ecological commitment, as he beautifully pointed out in the Message for World Day of Creation in September 2020:

> We repeat that the environmental activities of the Ecumenical Patriarchate are an extension of its ecclesiological self-consciousness and do not comprise a simple circumstantial reaction to a new phenomenon. The very life of the Church is an applied ecology.[1]

The Church of Rome more decisively joined the quest for the protection of our planet with the encyclical *Laudato Si'* in 2015, in which, among other things, Pope Francis openly acknowledges the leadership of our "beloved Ecumenical Patriarch Bartholomew" (LS, §7–9), showing a sense of continuity between his encyclical letter and the work of the patriarchate.

Our joint ecological action has strengthened our ecumenical bond and made us speak with one voice: we need to do more and go further together. As Pope Francis invites us in *Laudato Si'*, we need to open "a new dialogue about how we are shaping the future of our planet," "a conversation which includes everyone, since the environmental challenge we are undergoing, and its human roots, concern and affect us all" (LS, §14).

The unprecedented ecological crisis can indeed become a great opportunity for us to forge a new alliance of faiths to preserve the future of our planet. The invitation to a religious alliance and

---

1 Ecumenical Patriarch Bartholomew, "Message for World Day of Creation," Vatican News, September 1, 2020. https://www.vaticannews.va/en/church/news/2020-09/bartholomew-i-message-for-world-day-of-creation-full-text.html.

commitment for the environment became a public pledge last October 4, 2021, with the launch of the Faith Plans for People and Planet Program, where religious leaders from the major faiths signed, at the Vatican, the boldest environmental initiative to date by the global faith community.

The Focolare Movement is deeply committed to ecological conversion through practical action as well as through fostering dialogue with everyone for the protection of our planet. Stimulated by our General Assembly in early 2021, we have decided to take bold action through the creation of an ecological plan within our communities to bring about change and make our lives and our activities more sustainable.

Today, all our hopes for the environment seem to have been placed solely on science and technology. That is clearly very important. However, it is necessary to find, beside human intellect, other resources that can help us decide the path on which we want to walk as humanity today. Spiritual values that are still vital in driving individual and communitarian behavior can help us motivate a much-needed ecological and anthropological conversion. Above all, reconnecting our spiritual values to our ecological action reminds us that "rather than a problem to be solved, the world is a joyful mystery to be contemplated with gladness and praise" (LS, §12).

In this perspective, sustaining the future of our planet together can become a universal invitation, a space for encounter and cooperation between world religions and people of good will alike.

In *Laudato Si'*, the word "love" is used in the text seventy times so as to indicate a path on which everyone is invited to walk. Only by "being love," in fact, can humanity restore that gaze on itself and on the rest of creation to rediscover the golden thread of love that connects all beings, because, as Chiara Lubich reminds us, "on earth everything is in a relationship of love with everything else: each thing with each thing. But we need to be Love in order to find the golden thread of love between beings."[2]

In renewing the Focolare Movement's concrete commitment to an ecological conversion where—I must say—our young people are in the forefront, I wish for all of you that these days of reflection mark an important stage toward a renewed communion in action, prayer, and the search for new ways to care for creation and thus ensure a future of peace and fraternity for all.

---

2 Chiara Lubich, *Scritti spirituali*, vol. 1 (Rome: Città Nuova, 1997).

KEYNOTE ADDRESS

Ecumenical Patriarch Bartholomew

It is a joy for us to welcome you all to the "queen of cities" for the fifth Halki Summit of the Ecumenical Patriarchate, which this year is jointly organized and sponsored by our beloved Sisters of the Focolare Movement and specifically its Sophia University Institute.

It is indeed a privilege to address the theme of our gathering about "sustaining the future of the planet together" with an educational and religious school that features a unique ecumenical chair dedicated to our venerable predecessor, Ecumenical Patriarch Athenagoras, and the charitable founder of the Focolare, Chiara Lubich. Both of these visionaries of our respective churches established invaluable ecumenical relations, which have only been strengthened and sealed over the past years. Today we are honored to have among us the current president of the Focolare Movement and Vice Chancellor of Sophia University Institute as well as its Rector, Professor Giuseppe Argiolas. Thank you for gracing us with your presence and participation.

The focus of this summit is the comparative study of the ecological teachings and programs initiated—separately and in common—by our beloved brother Pope Francis in the Roman Catholic Church and our modesty in the Orthodox Church. For this reason, it is indeed a gift to have among us the recently-appointed Nuncio, Archbishop Marek Solczyński, who has made the presence of His Holiness at our humble summit very palpable through his personal message. We are deeply grateful for the voice of Pope Francis and the presence of the archbishop.

And like all of our initiatives—whether educational seminars, large-scale symposia, or these more concentrated summits—we have once again sought to include international, interdisciplinary, and ecumenical speakers and participants. This is because we are convinced that only together can we properly respond to and productively resolve the ecological crisis that humankind faces and the vital challenge to protect God's creation in our time. In this light, we would like to emphasize two key words in the title of our theme: namely "future" and "together."

Many of our speakers are educators who are committed to raising awareness and communicating knowledge to young people in our communities. This mission demonstrates the inseparable connection between our own generation and the generation of our children. We are responsible for the damage that we cause in our world. We are responsible for leaving behind a world that is sustainable for the future. We are responsible for shaping a world that our children can receive, respect, and transmit to their own children. And unfortunately it is true that we are the first generation that may leave behind a world that is in worse shape than the world we inherited. That is why the word "future" is critical.

The second word that we would underline is "together." It has become increasingly clear to us over the last decades—since the Ecumenical Patriarchate has emphasized that creation care is part and parcel of our vocation as Christians and our responsibility as human beings—that no single science or discipline, no single institution or individual, no single nation or organization, but also no single confession or religion can potentially appreciate all the diverse perspectives or possibly address all the various repercussions of the ecological crisis. This means that we cannot point fingers at any single cause, but we are obliged to hold hands in order together to assume responsibility for leaving the lightest footprint and bequeathing the least damage on the gift of creation.

In the "symbol of faith" shared by our "sister churches"—what our two churches both recognize and respect as the Nicaean Creed—we profess "one God, maker of heaven and earth, and of all things visible and invisible." This is a joint confession that we will celebrate together in just a few years, as we commemorate the 1700th anniversary since the convocation of that historical First Ecumenical Council that convened not very far from here. So beyond the scriptural teaching about our creator God who fashioned the world out of love and out of nothing, Christianity traditionally and doctrinally holds that all of creation is an inseparable part of our sacred identity and divine destiny.

By extension, then, every human action leaves a lasting imprint on the body of the earth. Human attitudes and behavior toward creation directly impact and reflect human attitudes and behavior toward other people as well as human conceptions about God. Ecology cannot be understood without reference to theology, just as it cannot be understood without reference to economy. At stake with the ecological crisis is not just our ability to live in a sustainable way, but our survival and our faith in God. Therefore, it becomes abundantly clear that only a cooperative and collective response—by religious leaders, informed scientists, political authorities, educational institutions, and financial organizations—will effectively be able to address these vital issues of our time.

At this point, we would like to remind you of two other concepts from Orthodox theology and spirituality that we have repeatedly emphasized in our effort to discern ways of promoting environmental awareness and action. The first of these words is "eucharist." In calling for a "eucharistic" spirit, the Orthodox Church is reminding us that the created world is not simply our personal possession, but rather it is a sacred gift—a gift from above, a gift of wonder and beauty. The proper response to such a gift is to accept and embrace it with gratitude and thanksgiving. This precludes any attempt at possessing or controlling the planet and its resources as human beings. In this respect, a eucharistic or sacramental worldview is the opposite of the way of selfish and wasteful consumption. Humans are called to be eucharistic beings—grateful to the Creator and respectful toward all creation.

The second word is "ascesis." The ascetic ethos or worldview is the intention and effort to protect the sacred gift of creation. It is the struggle for self-restraint and self-control, whereby we no longer willfully or wastefully consume every fruit, but instead manifest a sense of frugality and abstinence. Both of these attitudes of protection and self-restraint are expressions of love for God, humanity, and the natural creation. Only such love can protect the world from inevitable destruction.

However, what we would like to stress to you today is that, when we speak of eucharist and ascesis, we conventionally think of the ritual of liturgy and the way of monasticism. We would like to encourage you to think beyond the limited meaning of these terms, which have been burdened with many layers of ceremony and austerity through the centuries. Instead we would inspire you to consider these concepts as different ways of speaking about communion. Of course, "eucharist" is much more easily appreciated as a synonym for communion and sharing. But even "ascesis" is misinterpreted when we reduce it to an individualistic exercise. When we abstain from certain foods or luxuries or desires, we are conscious that our choices affect other people. We remember that those who have are counterbalanced by those who do not have. So even the ascetic worldview is another way of learning to share with other people and the rest of the world.

And here is where the vision of our brother Pope Francis coincides with the worldview we have proposed and promulgated for over thirty years. Both of us are convinced that what we do to our world "we do unto the least of our brothers and sisters" (Matt 25:50), just as what we do unto others we do to God Himself (Matt 25:45). It is no accident that, immediately after publishing his environmental encyclical *Laudato Si'*, the next encyclical issued by Pope Francis was *Fratelli Tutti*. And it is not by chance that, after numerous annual encyclicals since 1989 for the protection of the natural environment, the Ecumenical Patriarchate endorsed a document entitled *For the Life of the World*, which is about the social teaching of the Orthodox Church.

Both the pope and we recognize that the success of all our ecological activities is measured by the way we treat our fellow brothers and sisters, especially the poor. And the effectiveness of our response to the ecological crisis is assessed by the way we confront the social challenges of our world. Moreover, both the pope and we are fully aware that we can only address these issues together and not in isolation. This is why we have issued joint statements—along with the Archbishop of Canterbury—on the urgency of environmental sustainability, its impact on those living with poverty, and the importance of global cooperation.

So this is the paternal exhortation that we leave you with today as a signpost for your discussions over the next few days. Always remember that our vocation as Christians is about making and reinforcing *connections*:

- Connections between ourselves and all of God's creation
- Connections between our faith and our action, between our theology and our spirituality, between what we say and what we do
- Connections between science and religion, between our beliefs and every discipline
- Connections between our sacramental communion and our social consciousness
- Connections between our generation and the generations to come, just as between heaven and earth
- Connections between our two churches, but also with other churches and other faith communities

Because whenever we narrow our perception of life to ourselves, we overlook our vocation to transform the whole world. And creation provides a unique opportunity for all of us—normally so divided—to look beyond ourselves in order to address a common challenge and task that we must face together. That is precisely why we collaborate so closely with Pope Francis. And that is the shared service that we pray that you will support, that you will imitate, and that you will advance in your own lives and ministries. May God bless you all.

II. THEOLOGICAL PERSPECTIVES

1. THE IMPRINT OF THE CREATOR: GOD THE TRINITY IN CREATION

Piero Coda

1. Pope Francis and Patriarch Bartholomew call for an "ecological conversion." In saying this, they show us with vigor and clarity that, without further ado, there is a need today to change direction in the journey of humanity to promote a correct use of technology and a fraternal and supportive lifestyle in the ethos and praxis with which we inhabit and manage the common home. Failure to do so will result in the collapse of the social and environmental ecosystem.

But they do not stop there: for the root of this conversion is found in the human heart, and the human heart becomes new when it is reached and transformed by God's love. Once again, and with unprecedented urgency, the invitation is to be open to God's promise made through the prophet Ezekiel, that became an event of grace in the fullness of time, once and for all (ἐφάπαξ), in Christ Jesus: "A new heart I will give you, and a new spirit I will put within you; and I will remove from your body the heart of stone and give you a heart of flesh. I will put my spirit within you, and make you follow my statutes and be careful to observe my ordinances" (Ez 36:26–27).

It is the breath of the new Spirit that comes from God and fills the universe that humanity and the whole of creation await and invoke, even without knowing it, "with inexpressible groans": because, writes the Apostle Paul in his letter to the Romans, "For the creation waits with eager longing for the revealing of the children of God; that the creation itself will be set free from its bondage to decay and will obtain the freedom of the glory of the children of God" (Rom 8:19, 21).

2. Only "the encounter with the living and personal God: Father, Son and Holy Spirit," Patriarch Bartholomew writes, "can sustain the world";[3] "truth is contemplated, not understood on an intellectual level; God is seen, not examined on a theoretical level. Beauty is perceived, not conjectured abstractly."[4] Pope Francis echoes him in *Laudato Si'*: "The rich heritage of Christian spirituality, the fruit of twenty centuries of personal and communal experience, has a precious contribution to make to the renewal of humanity. ... A commitment this lofty cannot be sustained by doctrine alone, without a spirituality capable of inspiring us" (§216).

---

3 Ecumenical Patriarch Bartholomew, *Incontro al mistero* (Magnano: Edizioni Qiqajon, 2013), 74, 87.
4 Ecumenical Patriarch Bartholomew, *Grazia cosmica, umile preghiera: La visione ecologica del patriarca ecumenico di Costantinopoli Bartolomeo I*, ed. John Chryssavgis (Florence: Libreria Editrice Fiorentina, 2007), 189.

The key to ecological conversion, the grace and responsibility of which are contained in the gospel and which the Church is called to radiate, walking along the paths of life side by side with all those who, in different ways, are animated by the Spirit of God, is the contemplation of God the Trinity in creation through Christ Jesus, whose fullness (πλήρωμα), in the light (δόξα) and power (δύναμις) of the Holy Spirit, "is fulfilled in all things" (Eph 1:23: τὸ πλήρωμα τοῦ τὰ πάντα ἐν πᾶσιν πληρουμένου). This is the soul, dilated to the measure of the heart of God (cf. 1 John 3:20), which is called to give health, harmony, and beauty to the body of humanity and the cosmos in the dizzying breadth and depth in which it has expanded today.

Henri Bergson intuited this in the first half of the last century in his *Les deux sources de la morale et de la religion*. Even taking into account the degree of development achieved by technology in his time—and which today has gone to then unthinkable limits—the philosopher wrote: "Nature, by endowing us with an essentially creative intelligence, had prepared for us a certain enlargement," and the "machines," the fruit of human ingenuity, "have come to give our organism such a vast extension and such formidable power, so disproportionate to its size," that "in this disproportionately enlarged body, the soul remains what it was, now too small to fill it, too weak to lead it."[5]

---

5 Henri Bergson, *Les deux sources de la morale et de la religion* (1932), Italian translation (Milan: Edizioni di Comunità, 1947).

3. Therefore, to dilate and strengthen the soul, to the point of being in the *koinonía* of the Holy Spirit (2 Cor 13:13), "one heart and one soul" (cf. Acts 4:32): to expand it to the measure of the greater, but all too often wounded body of the universal human family and the entire cosmos. This is what is asked of us today as disciples of Jesus.

But what does it mean and how can it be achieved?

This becomes possible—this is the teaching, at the school of the one Master, listening to the Word of God and Christian Tradition, which Pope Francis and Patriarch Bartholomew offer us—when the soul opens its eyes to meet God's loving gaze and is transfigured by it: the gaze with which the Father contemplates in Christ Jesus, crucified and risen, in the drama of history lived in the light of the promise, the making of the "new heavens" and the "new earth," where God will be "all in all" (1 Cor 15:28).

What we have so many times left on the roadside as disciples of Jesus, and which Pope Francis and Patriarch Bartholomew invite us to rekindle, is first and foremost this grace: the fact that we can look in a new, contemplative and performative way at others and at the world, because first, and always again, we allow ourselves to be surprised by the gaze of measureless love with which God Himself looks at us: "You spare all things, for they are yours, O Lord, you who love the living" (Wis 11:25–27).

The decisive question of our time is a question of vision. Ecological conversion can only be born and nourished by a conversion of the gaze and a mystagogical education of the vision. The development of rational thought, of the sciences, of technology over the centuries of modernity—without us even realizing it—with all the precious gains it has brought with it, has however risked gradually turning our gaze away from the horizon of Light in which it lights up, penetrating the truth of things with wonder and gratitude, and judging with rectitude to make us act according to the measure of justice and love. *This is the gaze that originates from another gaze: that of the Creator and Lord of all things, that of God the Trinity.*

4. *The human being, in fact, knows because they are known.* Echoing Psalm 139, the Latin liturgy sings: "Before I was born, my God, you knew me." Human beings' knowledge is that of the ones who know themselves as creatures: the knowledge, that is, of the ones who discover, awakening to the miracle of life, that they are created "in the image and likeness of God," the Most High, the thrice Holy One (cf. Gen 14:22 and Isa 6:3). That is why, from time immemorial, man and woman through the wonders of creation have known—even if here in the twilight of what is not ultimate but only penultimate—the unfading Light of the mystery of God that floods, envelops, sustains, and promotes creation on its way to the homeland.

Humankind contemplates the imprint of the Creator in creation when they discover themselves as known and lovingly willed by the Creator as His creatures, in the depths of their being and in all the expressions of their existence. Even if this knowledge remains veiled, it is fragile, it can be obscured and even forgotten. Until He came, the Christ, the Son of God, who by becoming flesh (cf. John 1:14) became, in everything but sin, the son of man. It is He who forever dissolved darkness into Light: "No one knows the Son except the Father, and no one knows the Father except the Son and anyone to whom the Son chooses to reveal Him" (Matt 11:27).

Jesus is the dazzling testimony of this: He is Son because He is known (begotten) by God who is Father. His being is all and only enclosed and expressed in His being known to the Father as the Son (ὁμοούσιος τῷ Πατρὶ, confesses the first Ecumenical Council of Nicaea: of the same substance as the Father). It is in this way that He in turn knows the Father and communicates this knowledge to humankind by sharing with them the Spirit that He has received from the Father: "And because you are children, God has sent the Spirit of His Son into our hearts, crying, 'Abba! Father!'" (Gal 4:6). As Saint Irenaeus of Lyons teaches, "the knowledge of the Father is the Son, and the knowledge of the Son of God is brought about through the Holy Spirit."[6]

5. The event of the Incarnation, which is fulfilled in the Passover in which the Son gives His life to take it anew (cf. John 10:17), delivering "without measure" (John 3:34) the Spirit (cf. John

---

6 Cf. Irenaeus of Lyons, *Demonstration of Apostolic Preaching* 4–10.

19:30) to the brethren, reveals and brings to fulfilment the truth, goodness, and beauty of creation: "All things came into being through Him, and without Him not one thing came into being" (John 1:2); "He Himself is before all things, and in Him all things hold together" (Col 1:16-17).

Having been made partakers by grace of Christ's divine sonship, and illuminated by the light (δόξα) poured out by the Holy Spirit, we receive Christ's own gaze, His thought (νοῦς) (cf. 1 Cor 2:16): so that we can not only know God through His creatures, as in a clear reflection in which the Sun is mirrored, but we are introduced to knowing creatures in the interiority of the life of the Holy Trinity—as if received into a vortex of love—with the gaze of God Himself. Saint John of the Cross, the mystic Doctor, writes:

> The soul then sees how all heavenly and earthly creatures have their life and duration in God .... Even if it is true that the soul in such a state sees how these things, insofar as they are created, are distinct from God and discerns them in Him with all their strength, root and vigour, nevertheless so profound is the knowledge it has of God, as of Him who eminently contains all these things in His being, that it knows them better in the divine being than in itself. This is the great delight of such an awakening: to know creatures through God and not God through creatures.[7]

---

7 John of the Cross, *The Living Flame of Love* B, str. 4, 5, in idem, *Opere* (Rome, 1979), 823–824.

This describes, certainly, a singular mystical grace, of which there are many marvellous testimonies in the great Christian tradition of contemplation and holiness, in the East as well as in the West. But the *conversion of the gaze*—the "awakening," Saint John of the Cross calls it—brought about by the faith that makes us be and live in Christ in the love of the Holy Trinity, opens up access for all to this new gaze on creation. So that it *is Christ in us who looks at it contemplating it and walking in it and with it.*

6. But how does Christ look at and contemplate creation, Christ in us? As God's gift; as woven into a web of *relationships* in which creatures are made sharers in the life of God the Trinity; as actively involved in the labor pains of an immense birth, which is Christ's paschal life dilated to the measure of humanity and the cosmos.

Just a few words about each of these rays of new and intense light that are projected, in the Holy Spirit, by the gaze of Christ crucified and risen upon creation: each of them unveils a sapiential horizon of extraordinary significance also for the cosmological, scientific, and technological interpretation of reality.

7. First of all, that Christ's gaze contemplates creation as a *gift from God*. Describing the meaning and purpose of human activity

in the universe, the Second Vatican Council teaches in the Pastoral Constitution *Gaudium et Spes*:

> All human activity, constantly imperiled by man's pride and deranged self-love, must be purified and perfected by the power of Christ's cross and resurrection. For redeemed by Christ and made a new creature in the Holy Spirit, man is able to love the things themselves created by God, and ought to do so. He can receive them from God and respect and reverence them as flowing constantly from the hand of God. Grateful to his Benefactor for these creatures, using and enjoying them in detachment and liberty of spirit, man is led forward into a true possession of them, as having nothing, yet possessing all things. "All are yours, and you are Christ's, and Christ is God's" (1 Cor. 3:22-23). (§37)

The divine logic underlying creation is the astonishing logic of gift. And such is interpreted, welcomed, and promoted by humanity when it is enlightened and managed according to its original purpose: everything is created as a gift for each and for everyone, and each is created as a gift for each and for everyone. "In all knowledge and in every act of love," writes Pope Benedict XVI in *Caritas in Veritate*, "the human soul experiences a 'more' that closely resembles a gift received, a height to which we feel elevated" (§77).

Hence an attitude not of possession but of poverty and sobriety, not of idolatry but of freedom and sharing. Creatures—the Church's social doctrine teaches—have a universal destination: they are not for the privileged few, but for everyone, no one excluded. This is the "golden rule" of social, economic, and political behavior, its "first principle" (cf. *Laudato Si'*, 93; *Laborem Exercens*, 19). Created things are not mere instruments to be used (*uti*): but, contemplated as a gift in their arising, in the present, from the hands of God, they are to be welcomed and enjoyed (*frui*) in the doxological spirit of praise, thanksgiving, and communion.

8. But here is a further, astounding horizon of contemplation: in Christ's gaze, creation is no longer looked at from the outside but from within, recognizing the countless relationships that bind all creatures together in harmony (cf. *Laudato Si'*, §220). The tradition of Christian theology and spirituality has constantly and marvellously illuminated the imprint of this Trinitarian and Trinitized dynamic that is present in every creature and in the relationship that different creatures experience in relation to one another. This is how Chiara Lubich describes it, in a few lines of dazzling mystical intensity:

> In Creation everything is Trinity: Trinity the things themselves, because their Being is Love, is Father; the Law in them is Light, is Son, Word; Life in them is Love, is Holy Spirit. The All participated in the Nothing.

And they are Trinity with each other, for the one is of the other Son and Father, and all concur, loving each other, to the One, from whence they came forth.

And this through the man who indwells in Holy Communion.

Yes, everything converges and is brought into God through the Eucharist. The Eucharist, Maurice Blondel understood, is the "substantial bond" of the universe: Christ's becoming "all in all" through His given body and His shed blood, which is communicated to all and in all through the fruit of the earth and of man's labor. In the words of Jesus: "Just as the living Father sent me, and I live because of the Father (διά: by virtue of), so whoever eats me will live because of me" (John 6:57). The Eucharist "is in itself an act of cosmic love" (*Laudato Si'*, §236).

Thanks to this, the vocation of the human person is realized. Pope Francis writes: "The human person grows more, matures more and is sanctified more to the extent that he or she enters into relationships, going out from themselves to live in communion with God, with others and with all creatures. In this way, they make their own that trinitarian dynamism which God imprinted in them when they were created" (*Laudato Si'*, §240).

Then—as Francis of Assisi sang after the experience of identification with Christ Crucified lived at La Verna, which made him contemplate the world with God's eyes of love—one recognizes and treats as brothers and sisters not only human persons, but all creatures: the sun, the moon, the stars, the wind, water, fire, mother earth. Francis enters into dialogue with all creatures and, as Thomas of Celano narrates, even preaches to birds and flowers, inviting them "to praise and love God, as beings endowed with reason."[8]

> The ultimate purpose of other creatures is not to be found in us. Rather, all creatures are moving forward with us and through us towards a common point of arrival, which is God, in that transcendent fullness where the risen Christ embraces and illumines all things. (*Laudato Si'*, §83)

9. A piercing, dramatic, often tragic and, at first glance, insurmountable question remains in the background: what about suffering, misery, defeat, failure, death?

If Christ is not risen in vain is our faith (cf. 1 Cor 15:17). But the wisdom (σοφία) and power (δύναμις) of God, which shine forth in the resurrection, flow from Christ crucified (cf. 1 Cor 1:22–24). This is not only a spiritual and religious truth: it is an onto-logical truth and therefore—at its own level and with its own specific way of expression—it is an anthropological, ethical, and cosmological truth. The ecological conversion of the gaze is called to penetrate, in depth, with faith and daring, into the unprecedented horizon disclosed by the Easter of Jesus' death and resurrection, also in discerning and dealing with what hinders and opposes the path of life and love.

---

8   Thomas of Celano, *First Life of St. Francis*, XXIX, 81: 660.

Is it not Jesus Himself, looking at the Trinitarian law of life that is love inscribed in nature, who illuminates the transforming and divinizing dynamic of what takes place in His Passover by referring to the grain of wheat that, falling into the ground, bears much fruit (John 12:24)? and to the woman who, "when she gives birth, is in pain, because her hour has come; but when she has given birth to the child, she no longer remembers the suffering, for joy that a man has come into the world" (John 16:21)?

By directing our gaze, through Christ crucified and risen, with discretion, fear of God, humility, and tenderness, into this mysterious but real horizon of meaning, we can perceive something of the paschal dynamic of God's love that makes its way through the troubled process involving human history and the entire cosmos, as Paul describes it in his letter to the Romans:

> We know that the whole creation has been groaning in labor pains until now; and not only the creation, but we ourselves, who have the first fruits of the Spirit, groan inwardly while we wait for adoption, the redemption of our bodies. For in hope we were saved. (Rom 8:22–24a)

Suffering, trial, tragedy, death are already being redeemed in Christ crucified and risen and can become, through our compassion, an expression and instrument of a greater love: made of mercy, solidarity, justice, hope, new life, according to the words of the Apostle Paul: "I am now rejoicing in my sufferings for your sake, and in my flesh I am completing what is lacking in Christ's afflictions for the sake of his body, that is, the church" (Col 1:24).

There is a close relationship, no longer detachable, between the cry of the poor and the cry of the earth (cf. *Laudato Si'*, §49). The Word (λόγος) of God became Himself a cry, this cry, every cry, on the wood of the cross: "a cry that says at the same time the triumph of God's love and the truth and depth of His incarnation."[9]

10. *Ecological conversion is first and foremost conversion of outlook*: this is the message that Pope Francis and Patriarch Bartholomew address to us in a wonderful and fascinating symphony.

Assuming the gift, responsibility, and creativity of this gaze of wisdom and mercy in Christ, one can and must undertake, with spirit and realism, constructive paths of dialogue with the philosophical, scientific, and technical interpretation of creation: with regard to the great ethical questions that challenge the human conscience today regarding the mystery of life, as well as with regard to the appropriate techniques for a sustainable and fraternal promotion of social and environmental development.

This is not simply a utopia, nor merely an ethical imperative. Faith in Christ states that this gaze is the expression of an ontological event that happened "once and for all" and that continually recurs: when from the heart, tacit or expressed, Mary's readiness to the

---

9 Marie-Eugène de l'Enfant Jésus, *Je veux voir Dieu* (Venasque: Ed. du Carmel, 1998), 1016.

angel's surprising announcement blossoms in us, through the tender and strong impulse of the Holy Spirit: "γένοιτό μοι κατὰ τὸ ῥῆμά σου" (Luke 1:38).

Then, with Mary, everything in Christ crucified and risen is transfigured: as the Church of the East sings in the hymn *Akathistos*, addressing Mary, χώρα τοῦ Θεοῦ τοῦ ἀχοράτου: "You bear Him who sustains all things. Hail, O star, precursor of the Sun; Hail, O womb of the God who becomes incarnate. Hail, through Thee is creation renewed."[10]

---

10 Author's translation.

2. WHY ECO-DOGMATICS MATTERS FOR ECO-PRAXIS: AN EASTERN ORTHODOX PERSPECTIVE

Nikolaos Asproulis

The Climate Crisis as a Global Crisis:
Setting the Contemporary Scene

The climate crisis is considered nowadays the most urgent threat facing humanity. As a complex problem, comprised of a variety of dimensions—such as CO_2 emissions, global warming, large-scale shifts in weather patterns, meat production models, biodiversity loss, sea pollution from plastics, even mega-fires—it puts the entire environment at risk, endangering the very survival of the human species and the natural world.

Rooted in an ego-centric interpretation, dominant from the Enlightenment to this day, of the biblical account of the creation of the world,[11] humanity has adopted a lifestyle that assumes a

---

[11] Gen 1–2; for instance, 2:15: "The Lord God took the man and put him in the Garden of Eden to work it and take care of it."

controlling role and position within the world. It was the major Enlightenment thinkers, and particularly René Descartes's (1596–1650) "cogito ergo sum," which led to the gradual disassociation of humanity from the materiality of the world, establishing a worldview which presents human beings as the "the lord(s) and possessor(s) of nature" in Descartes's own words.[12]

It was only in 1967 that Lynn White Jr. highlighted the historical responsibility of Christianity for this outlook, thus bringing to the fore the spiritual and religious aspects of the ecological problem in addition to the economic and political, all of which still prevail today.[13] In the same vein, Metropolitan of Pergamon John Zizioulas (1931–2023), the primary spokesman of the Ecumenical Patriarchate's eco-theological vision, would be among the first who quite early turned our attention to White's detailed demonstration of the historical responsibility of Judeo-Christian theology for the environmental crisis.[14]

The climate crisis is not a condition that threatens a piece of land far away from one's own home. It puts at risk one's own villages and cities, causing incalculable problems to the local environment, climate, and economy. It goes without saying then that the climate crisis not only challenges the whole planet, but also affects it in

---

12 René Descartes, *Discours de la Méthode*, part VI. https://www.bartleby.com/34/1/6.html (accessed November 2, 2022).

13 Lynn Townsend White, Jr., "The Historical Roots of Our Ecologic Crisis," *Science* 155, no. 3767 (March 10, 1967): 1203–1207.

14 Cf. John Chryssavgis and Nikolaos Asproulis, eds., *Priests of Creation: John Zizioulas on Discerning an Ecological Ethos* (London: T&T Clark, 2021), 61, 74, 96.

different ways, and that something should be done to reduce its consequences.

Recent Secular Initiatives

Against this background, how have people, governments, and Christian churches responded?

In recent years, certain important initiatives have been put into practice by political leaders of the global community in an attempt to deal with the problem. Among the major initiatives, we should note the "Paris Agreement" of 2015. Among the ambitious decisions to be implemented in the following years were "holding the increase in the global average temperature to well below 2°C above pre-industrial levels and pursuing efforts to limit the temperature increase to 1.5°C above pre-industrial levels, recognizing that this would significantly reduce the risks and impacts of climate change."[15]

In a similar vein, the "European Green Deal: Towards a Climate Neutral EU by 2050," recently issued by the European Commission (2019), sought to transform our everyday lives by suggesting certain and deeply transformative policies (e.g., modernization of the European economy, supplying clean and affordable energy, mobilizing industry for a clean economy, etc.) for a sustainable

---

15   The Paris Agreement, November 5, 2022, https://unfccc.int/sites/default/files/english_paris_agreement.pdf.

future, taking into account, at least in principle, the importance of leaving no one behind in the transition.[16]

Religious Initiatives: Orthodox Christianity Goes Green

Not only governments and organizations but also Christian churches decided to align their efforts to address the climate crisis. In this regard, one should give special attention to Pope Francis' Encyclical *Laudato Si'*, released in 2015, a result of a consultation of experts from all over the world, which appeals for "a new dialogue about how we are shaping the future of our planet. We need a conversation which includes everyone, since the environmental challenge we are undergoing, and its human roots, concern and affect us all."[17]

In this direction one can also refer to the Joint Statement of Pope Francis, Patriarch Bartholomew, and the Archbishop of Canterbury, released in September 2021, which "call(s) on everyone, whatever their belief or worldview, to endeavour to listen to the cry of the earth and of people who are poor, examining their behaviour and

---

16 "European Green Deal," November 7, 2022, https://ec.europa.eu/info/strategy/priorities-2019-2024/european-green-deal_en.

17 Pope Francis, *Laudato Si'*, November 2, 2022, https://www.vatican.va/content/francesco/en/encyclicals/documents/papa-francesco_20150524_enciclica-laudato-si.html. For an Orthodox reception of the Encyclical see Metropolitan John Zizioulas, "Pope Francis' Encyclical *Laudato Si'*," in *Ecotheology, Climate Justice and Food Security*, ed. Dietrich Werner-Elizabeth Geglitza (Geneva: Globethics.net, 2016), 179–186.

pledging meaningful sacrifices for the sake of the earth which God has given us."[18]

But what about Eastern Orthodoxy? Although not transformed into a political program, the care of creation has always found a central place in Orthodoxy's theological vision and monastic life. It was only after the modern explosion of the climate crisis that this vision started to take shape as a specific strategy of the Ecumenical Patriarchate in its effort to increase people's awareness on a global scale. In this light, the Ecumenical Patriarchate, under the guidance of the late Patriarch Demetrios and the current Patriarch Bartholomew, organized a series of international meetings, conferences, consultations, and publications, where representatives of the world religions, as well as scientists and world leaders, gathered together to reflect on the urgent issue of the climate crisis. One could refer here to the conference held in Patmos in September 23–25, 1988 on the topic "Revelation and the Future of Humanity"; the decision to declare September 1 as a prayer day for all Orthodox Churches within the jurisdiction of the Ecumenical Patriarchate; the series of special ecological seminars which took place at the Theological School of Halki (Halki Island,

---

18 Ecumenical Patriarch Bartholomew, Pope Francis, and Archbishop of Canterbury, "A Joint Message for the Protection of Creation," November 1, 2022, https://www.oikoumene.org/resources/documents/joint-statement-pope-francis-ecumenical-patriarch-bartholomew-and-archbishop-of-canterbury-urge-care-for-future-of-the-planet. For an Orthodox assessment of the statement see my "Un messaggio congiunto per la tutela del creato. Una riflessione ortodossa orientale," *Concilium* 58, no. 3 (2022): 151–155.

Turkey), on a wide range of topics, including "Environment and Religious Education" (1994), "Environment and Ethics" (1995), and "Environment and Communications" (1996); international symposia like "Revelation and the Environment" (1995) which took place on the historic and sacred island of Patmos, or "The Black Sea in Crisis" (1997); or the most recent, ninth international symposium on board ship, entitled "Toward a Greener Attica: Preserving the Planet and Protecting Its People."[19]

The goal of all these initiatives was to highlight: a) the urgency of the problem; b) the moral dimension of the crisis; c) the need for a universal response to the challenge, with a broad cooperation of all available powers (science, religions, technocrats, associations, individuals, etc.), so as to limit as far as possible the effects of the destruction of creation.

Towards this end, one should also refer to the following two important texts: a) *The Mission of the Orthodox Church in Today's World*, adopted by the Holy and Great Synod of Crete (2016) which stresses the role played by humanity in earth's destruction and its responsibility for the protection of the environment;[20] and b) *For the Life of the World: Towards a Social Ethos of the Orthodox Church*,

---

19 For more details on the Ecumenical Patriarchate's initiatives see John Chryssavgis, *Creation as Sacrament: Reflections on Ecology and Spirituality* (London: T&T Clark, 2019) and Ecumenical Patriarch Bartholomew, *In the World, Yet Not of the World: Social and Global Initiatives of Ecumenical Patriarch Bartholomew*, ed. John Chryssavgis (New York: Fordham University Press, 2010).
20 Holy and Great Council, *The Mission of the Orthodox Church in Today's World*, September 9, 2022, https://www.holycouncil.org/mission-orthodox-church-todays-world.

authored by a special commission of Orthodox scholars appointed by Ecumenical Patriarch Bartholomew, which highlights the role and responsibility of the Orthodox Church, and the ontological interconnectedness of all creatures, while criticizing the political and economic causes of the present disaster.[21]

Inspired by Ecumenical Patriarch Bartholomew's enormous work, the Volos Academy for Theological Studies[22] has cooperated with WWF Greece in order to achieve the core strategic objective of the theory of change, namely to encourage and motivate Orthodox leaders from select Balkan countries to be champions for coal phase-out and climate action. This initiative resulted in a major publication entitled *The Orthodox Church Addresses the Climate Crisis*,[23] as well as a wider project, consisting of various activities embedded in a local parish (the Annunciation of Theotokos, Evaggelistria, Nea Ionia, Volos, Greece) like a series of public lectures for the wider audience on timely environmental issues, webinars, radio broadcasts, and blog posts.[24] In addition, a major international climate justice e-conference was co-organized in October 2021, under the general theme: "Best practices of the Orthodox Church for addressing the climate crisis, in view of the

---

21 *For the Life of the World: Towards a Social Ethos of the Orthodox Church*, June 15, 2022, https://www.goarch.org/el/social-ethos.
22 For a general overview of the activities and agenda of the Volos Academy for Theological Studies, visit its official website at www.acadimia.org.
23 Theodota Nantsou and Nikolaos Asproulis, eds., *The Orthodox Church Addresses the Climate Crisis* (Athens/Volos: Volos Academy Publications, 2021).
24 https://www.acadimia.org/ylopoiimena-programmata/prasini-enoria (accessed November 19, 2022).

UNFCCC COP26." The conference revolved around the presentation of potential best practices which take place in the various Orthodox Churches (with special emphasis on the Balkans) and which relate to specific actions in parishes and monasteries, encyclicals and decisions of local Churches, etc., aimed at raising public awareness and addressing the consequences of the climate crisis.[25]

The major objective of the second phase of the Volos initiative is the establishment of an Energy Community, with the aim of producing, consuming, and sharing between the members of the community the energy necessary to cover the needs of approximately fifteen legal bodies, with the possibility of expansion in the near future. In a wider context, this development is considered unique in kind (as an initiative by religious and faith bodies) and as a pilot program in the Greek context. Church engagement on green issues is not only of invaluable importance for the protection of the environment, but at the same time it is a journey of groups of people—not a list of moral commandments to blindly obey, but a lifelong journey that needs to unfold gradually.

Despite, however, the importance and the practical results of these initiatives, the majority of local Churches, parishes, theologians, and faithful still remain, if not indifferent towards the destabilization of the climate and environmental catastrophe, at least without the necessary tools with which to conceptualize a proper eco-theological vision and practice of how the rich

---

25 https://acadimia.org/ylopoiimena-programmata/prasini-enoria-vinteothiki (accessed November 22, 2022).

ecclesiastical tradition and doctrinal orthodoxy can relate to our modern concerns and especially to the survival of the earth. In the remainder of this chapter, this new way of theologizing will be outlined, as the necessary step to deal seriously and successfully with the climate crisis.

Towards a New Model of Doing Theology: Eco-Dogmatics

It is well known that dogmatics or dogmatic theology[26] is that area of theology dealing with the articulation, as well as the interpretation, of the theoretical truths of faith concerning God *ad intra* (*theologia*) and God *ad extra* (*oikonomia*). It is widely considered as the very core of Christian systematic theology, upon which all other theological disciplines are grounded.

But what about *eco-dogmatics*? This is not a new chapter of dogmatics. On the contrary, this neologism expresses the need to use *ecology* as a *contextual* method of doing theology in view of today's climate crisis. It is not just about *creation theology*, that is, an individual chapter of dogmatics which already exists in every traditional manual, but the underlying background that substantiates every single chapter of theology (its prerequisites, method, and perspective).

As a method, eco-dogmatics can make use of certain theoretical tools and assumptions of ecology, e.g., the movement of materials and energy through living communities, the successional

---

26 Cf. the definition of "Dogmatic Theology" in *Catholic Encyclopedia*, https://www.newadvent.org/cathen/14580a.htm (accessed November 8, 2022).

development of ecosystems, or the patterns of biodiversity and its effect on ecosystem processes.[27] With all these tools, which require a frank and open dialogue between (Orthodox) theology and science,[28] eco-dogmatics can approach in a new and constructive way certain aspects of doctrinal orthodoxy, such the Trinitarian, Christological, anthropological, sacramental, ecclesiological, and eschatological doctrines, giving them an *incarnational* dimension, badly needed today.

Patterns of Eco-Dogmatics: Eco-Christology

So what should we do? In more theological terms, "How does God want the world to survive?"[29] To this end various answers have been proposed over time.

On the one hand, there was the notion of the *immortality of the soul*, an idea which dominated the ancient Greek world. However, if anything offers creation the possibility of existing in a natural

---

27 For instance, "ecosystem" itself as a concept can be useful in literal or metaphorical terms for Trinitarian theology or the eucharistic experience and practice, since "an ecosystem is a geographic area where plants, animals, and other organisms, as well as weather and landscapes, work together to form a bubble of life." "Ecosystem," https://education.nationalgeographic.org/resource/ecosystem (accessed November 5, 2022).

28 Cf. for instance: Eftymios Nicolaidis, *Science and Eastern Orthodoxy: From the Greek Fathers to the Age of Globalization* (Baltimore: John Hopkins University Press, 2011); D. Buxhoeveden and Gayle Woloschak, eds., *Science and the Eastern Orthodox Church* (Farnham: Ashgate, 2011); Alexei V. Nesteruck, *Light from the East: Theology, Science and the Eastern Orthodox Tradition* (Minneapolis: Fortress Press, 2003).

29 John Zizioulas, "Preserving God's Creation," in idem, *The Eucharistic Communion and the World* (London: T&T Clark, 2011), 162.

way, it inevitably leads to an obligatory immortality. This is a view more or less shared today by romantics or even eco-activists, who strongly oppose any human interference to provide green solutions to the climate crisis, in favor of nature's capacity to secure its own existence and survival. On the other hand, equally unacceptable is a related solution based on *moral* or *juridical* foundations, supposing that the created being can improve itself by practicing or obeying divine, natural, or even human law. According to this view, creation can survive by putting into practice a certain political or cultural program. From a theological point of view, though, this is not the case: "No, death is not conquered like that. The only thing conquered is preoccupation with the problem of death,"[30] as Zizioulas clearly states.

Another way of thinking, or rather mode of life, is required here, which calls into question our given theological assumptions. Theology needs to appeal to the patristic concept of *hypostatic union*, which prioritizes Christ's personhood over His two natures, without, however, bringing them into opposition. It was particularly Maximus the Confessor (580–662), who, by working deeply along Christological lines, pointed out the need for a relationship between the created and the uncreated to overcome death. The human being was meant to assume this role. However, the Fall foiled this divinely ordained task, necessitating a change of the divine plan.

---

30 John Zizioulas, *Communion and Otherness: Further Studies in Personhood and the Church* (London: T&T Clark, 2006), 258.

What was required now was for the Logos to become human. But still, is this perception of the close relation between the created and uncreated in Christ sufficient to deal with the overturning of the catastrophic consequences of the climate crisis? It seems that another and further step is required here, which construes Christology in a "greener" way. To this end it needs to appeal to the concept of "deep incarnation."

At the heart of the deep incarnation perspective is a fresh reception and interpretation of the historical roots of doctrinal orthodoxy. It has been mainly formulated as a response to the liberal Christology developed by Friedrich Schleiermacher (1768–1834), according to whom God is fully present only in Jesus' divine consciousness, while humanity (meaning body and flesh) is considered as an instrument of sin and death, not of salvation. On the contrary, deep incarnation stresses the importance of both fleshliness (materiality) and human consciousness in Christ. Thus, it tries to combine the biology of growth, vulnerability, and decay, which characterize the created order, with religious awareness, creation in its entirety, and Jesus as a human individual, as a complete human being. In this respect, deep incarnation focuses not only on the person of Jesus, his personal history, but takes into consideration also the human, natural, and cultural environment of Jesus in its entirety, meaning his fellow Jews, his interlocutors (Samaritan people and others), other creatures (animals), as well as the fauna and flora of ancient Israel.

Although Protestant in its roots, deep incarnation has sound patristic and medieval parallels, in that it rightly sees Christ as the only mediator between created and uncreated, as the only person who has assumed the fullness of cosmic materiality, and finally, as the only condition for the entire planet to be ontologically saved.

Eco-Christian Anthropology: From *Imago Dei* to *Imago Mundi*

The time has come to focus on Christian anthropology and possible redefinitions from an ecological perspective. By redefining the image of God in a more inclusive way through the lens of "dinivanimality,"[31] theology can provide an all-embracing anthropology that accounts for the particular place and reception of animals, as well as all creatures and creation *in toto*, not only in our discourse, but also in our practice. If one defines the human from the standpoint of a personalist ontology,[32] then the human cannot be understood without a clear reference to a You and an It: "Every part of creation matters,"[33] or every single creature of God matters. The *imago Dei* is incomplete, unless the whole creation is recognized as being a constitutive part of it.

Such an inclusive understanding of *imago Dei* points, perhaps

---

31   Stephen Moore, ed., *Divinanimality: Animal Theory, Creaturely Theology* (New York: Fordham University Press, 2014).
32   I follow here John Zizioulas, *Being as Communion: Studies in Personhood and the Church* (New York: St. Vladimir's Seminary Press, 1985).
33   See Kees Nieuwerth, Peter Pavlovic, and Adrian Shaw, eds., *Every Part of Creation Matters*, Conference of European Churches 8 (Geneva: Globethics.net, 2022).

unconsciously, to the concept of *imago mundi*. By this, contemporary theologians[34] attempt to redefine human identity in light of the urgent climate crisis. If the image of God in humanity cannot be fully manifested without taking all creatures into account, this clearly means that animals, as well as the whole creation, do share in the salvation of the whole creation, and that they do participate in heaven. After all, this is the ultimate goal of the divine plan as it was finally realized through Christ's paschal mystery: the salvation (theosis) of the entire world, not only of humanity. Otherwise, the non-human creation would have been created in vain ("Man and beast thou savest, O Lord," Ps 36:6b), and the Pauline premises that the whole earth will be saved, and Christ will "unite all things in Him, things in heaven and things on earth" (Eph 1:9–10) would sound irrelevant.

In this vein, theological anthropology should ascribe priority to communion/relation as that dimension of the *imago* which points to the ontological affinity between all non-human creatures. In anthropology, it is the personalist and relational understanding of the human being that seeks to overcome the alleged fixed dichotomy between humanity and nature.

By Way of Conclusion

The climate crisis cannot be dealt with in a managerial way. As the ultimate evil of our era, it should be clearly understood as

---

34   Cf. Annelien C. Rabie-Boshoff, "Imago mundi: Justice of Peace," *HTS Teologiese Studies/Theological Studies* 78, no. 2 (2022): 1–7.

an existential problem, or rather as an "ecological sin," the fruit of human beings' disobedience to God's commandment to "preserve and take care" of the planet. We live in a critical time, where radical action is required against our egocentric lifestyle and consumerist culture that prevents us from finding a real meaning in life. To this end we need a theology that will take the risk of working closely and cooperating with the environmental sciences and ecology, and that will dive deeply its own tradition and use an *eco-theological hermeneutic* to bring to the fore those elements necessary to address the climate crisis. Both the long history of the Church and the initiatives described above have been nothing more than an attempt to cope with ecological evil and the disorder caused to creation, offering a new vision and practice in the framework of cosmological *theosis*, which remains the central goal of life in Christ.

3. ECO-THEOLOGY AND CHRISTIAN SPIRITUALITY: THE CONTRIBUTION OF THE "GREEN" ECUMENICAL PATRIARCH AND THE IMPORTANCE OF THE PAPAL ENCYCLICAL *LAUDATO SI'*

Augustinos Bairactaris

Introduction: Eco-Theology and Integrity of Creation

In his 1949 book *A Sand County Almanac*, Aldo Leopold offers the following terminology regarding the notion of integrity of creation:

> A thing is right when it tends to preserve the integrity, stability and beauty of the biotic community. It is wrong when it tends otherwise. ... Conservation is getting nowhere because it is incompatible with our Abrahamic concept of land. We abuse land because we regard it as a commodity belonging to us. When we see land as a community to which we belong, we may begin to use it with love and respect. There is no other way for land to survive the impact of mechanized man, or

for us to reap from it the esthetic harvest it is capable, under science, of contributing to culture. That land is a community is the basic concept of ecology, but that land is to be loved and respected is an extension of ethics.[35]

Integrity of creation was clarified by the WCC later in Glion during the 1987 meeting of the Church and Society Working Group, which stated: "It refers to the intrinsic and instrumental value of each creature in its relationship to its environment and to God."[36] In other words, the notion of integrity of creation is useful because: a) it has given a new perspective to the doctrine of creation and b) it has offered a context of justice and peace.[37] In fact, the task of that group was to conceptualize the interaction between theory and praxis in the field of society, technology, and environment, finding patterns of sustainable development which would avoid critical threats to the environment. Development is not only to be measured in terms of economic growth and statistics. Rather, development should be seen relative to quality of life. Holmes Rolston, a leading figure in environmental ethics, proposed a combination of *biocentric* and *ecocentric* approaches.[38] What matters is not only equality, but

---

35 Aldo Leopold, *A Sand County Almanac* (Oxford: Oxford University Press, 1949), 8.
36 *Report and Background Papers, Meeting of the Church and Society Working Group, Glion, Switzerland, September 1987* (Geneva: WCC, 1987), 37. See also, Peter Bakken, Joan Gibb Engel, and Ronald Engel, *Ecology, Justice and Christian Faith: A Critical Guide to the Literature* (London: Greenwood Press, 1995).
37 Niles Preman, *Resisting the Threats to Life: Covenanting for Justice, Peace and the Integrity of Creation* (Geneva: WCC, 1998), 58.
38 Andrew Light and Holmes Rolston, eds., *Environmental Ethics:An Anthology*

SUSTAINING THE FUTURE OF OUR PLANET TOGETHER

also quality. Also, the same working group declared that humans are part of a community of life, which forms a single interrelated system.[39] In that framework, the ecumenical movement through the activities of the World Council of Churches launched a project in 2013 in Busan, based upon the axioms of *eco-theology* and *climate justice*.[40]

The Ecumenical Work on Climate Change

Climate change and global warming are no longer issues discussed solely among scientists, but have extended beyond and far the scientific communities and the political world, reaching public opinion. Climate change has become one of the most important challenges that the global community faces today. Due to the initiatives of the UN, the WCC, the National and Regional Church Councils, scientific reports such as the Stern Review[41] and NASA research, and some prophetic spiritual leaders, such as Ecumenical Patriarch Bartholomew, a growing consensus on climate change has taken place.

Thus, it is evident that ecumenical concern about the climate crisis is not something new. On the contrary, the WCC, together

---

(Oxford: Blackwell Publishing, 2003), 143–153.

39 *Report and Background Papers, Meeting of the Church and Society Working Group, Glion, Switzerland, September 1987*, 42.

40 https://www.oikoumene.org/en/resources/documents/assembly/2013-busan/adopted-documents-statements/the-way-of-just-peace.

41 www.sigss.co.uk/stern-report.asp.

with a number of National and Regional Christian Councils and Forums, since the mid-1970s has been advocating for sustainable development as a part of the Justice, Peace, and Integrity of Creation conciliar process. That sustainable development should include sustainable agriculture, as well as protection and reasonable use of natural resources, such as water and forest products.[42]

The WCC started a program on climate change in 1988 based on the principles of sustainable development and responsible society. The main goal of that project was to assist churches on a global scale to take environmentally friendly actions, urging countries and international bodies, law and policy makers, and governments to be engaged in eco-justice initiatives.

Additionally, that project is deeply rooted in the biblical themes of *the wholeness of creation* and *commitment to justice.* Namely, the Bible teaches that life is created, sustained, and made whole by the power of God's Holy Spirit. God is the one who creates humans out of the dust of the earth, while sin breaks relationships among humankind and the rest of the creation. Particularly, the role of the Holy Spirit in creation was highlighted by the working group of WCC, since the life-giving Spirit reconciles, heals, liberates, and brings salvation to all. Secondly, there was mention of the special place of humanity within creation, according to the doctrine of

---

42 Guillermo Kerber, "Climate Change and Climate Justice: An Ecumenical Ethical Approach," in Andrianos Lucas, Jan-Willem Sneep, and Konstantinos Kenanidis, eds., *Ecological Theology and Environmental Ethics*, vol. 2 (Chania: Orthodox Academy of Crete, 2012), 233.

God's image and likeness. Thus, humanity is actually part of God's creation and not its master. Thirdly, the program emphasized the biblical origins of humanity out of the soil, a sign of the bond of unity between humanity and the earth. Fourthly, the Sabbath feast is referred to the whole creation, as a sign of rest.[43]

It is beyond any doubt that God entrusted creation to humans not to exploit it, but to care for and guard it,[44] because everything was made and has been sustained in life by God's providence. Accordingly, humans must treat the earth with trust. Unfortunately, the understanding of the human being created in the image of God gave rise to a false anthropocentric supremacy over and against nature.[45] The consequence of this is the current ecological crisis, which in fact describes the disharmony between humans and creation; therefore, Christian churches must reexamine their view of God, humanity, and nature.[46]

Humans' arrogance and lust for "absolute freedom" from their Creator led humanity to a sinful autonomy and alienation from both

---

43 Daniel Kwame Bediako, "The Biblical Sabbatical Year and Its Implications for Ecology: An Exegesis of Exodus 23:10-11," in Andrianos Lucas, Jan-Willem Sneep, and Konstantinos Kenanidis, eds., *Ecological Theology and Environmental Ethics*, vol. 2 (Chania: Orthodox Academy of Crete, 2012), 178.

44 Christina Manohar, "Toward a Mission Theology of Environment," in Krickwin Marak and Atul Aghamkar, eds., *Ecological Challenges and Christian Mission* (New Delhi: CMS/ISPCK, 1998).

45 Gen 3:20: "Adam was given responsibility to manage." See also, Ps 115:15–16: "To protect and take care of creation."

46 T. Milley, *Living in the Environment* (California: Wadsworth, 1992), 65.

God and nature. So, the human being by setting himself at the very center of life ignored God and exploited all things materialistically, exercising a destructive dominion.[47]

Similarly, the notion of eco-justice is not only an ethical issue, but it is a complex theological subject, which reflects upon the rights of the poor, the orphans, the strangers, and the widows of the Bible who do not have the means to overcome or to adapt to climate change. God is the One who does what is just, cares, and gives security to the poor.[48] All these people represent the vulnerable communities to whom Jesus said in His Sermon on the Mount: "Blessed are you who are poor, for yours is the Kingdom of God. ... Blessed are those who are hungry and thirsty for justice" (Matt 5:3ff).

Ecumenical Patriarch Bartholomew Advocating Care for God's Creation: "Humans Are Stewards, Not Proprietors of Land"

Ecumenical Patriarch Bartholomew has become worldwide known for his efforts (Halki environmental educational seminars, international scientific symposia on world rivers and seas, etc.) to increase people's environmental awareness to care and protect the environment, their own home, and to convince political leaders to take measures to preserve life on earth. His efforts and achievements

---

47 Pramod Ramteke, "Ecological Crisis: The Biblical Perspective," in Andrianos Lucas, Jan-Willem Sneep, and Konstantinos Kenanidis, eds., *Ecological Theology and Environmental Ethics*, vol. 2 (Chania: Orthodox Academy of Crete, 2012), 126.
48 Central Committee on Climate Change and the World Council of Churches, *Minute on Global Warming and Climate Change* (Geneva: WCC, 2010), 22.

have earned him the honorific title of "Green Patriarch." Every September 1 is the day when all Orthodox Churches address prayers and supplications for the well-being of God's good creation, since that date has been established as the Day for the Protection of the Natural Environment. Also, in 2007 in Sibiu, Romania, the 3rd European Ecumenical Assembly established the initiative "Time for Creation," from September 1 to October 4.[49]

Ecumenical Patriarch Bartholomew has always respected the sanctity of nature along with the freedom of the person. Moreover, he speaks about the virtue of *reconciliation* of humankind with its physical surroundings, which represents a spiritual event.[50] Therefore, human freedom must be connected to responsibility toward creation. However, humans have mostly failed in this cause to participate in God's creation, because modern society values production over human dignity and wealth over human integrity.[51]

Furthermore, he has made important contributions to the development of an ecological Magna Carta, offering an Orthodox witness in the modern world. He constantly encourages the faithful and not-faithful members of local communities to behave with gentleness and love to the earth, showing the inner connection between humanity and creation. He invites people of good will to

---

49 http://www.oikoumene.org/en/events-sections/countdown-to-climate-justice/time-forcreation.html.
50 Message of Ecumenical Patriarch Bartholomew, Message on the "Day of Prayer for the Protection of all Creation," September 1, 1996.
51 Message of Ecumenical Patriarch Bartholomew, Message on the "Day of Prayer for the Protection of all Creation," September 1, 1994.

participate in his environmental vision, because he believes strongly that all people, regardless of their race, language, culture, or faith, must cooperate in order to secure the safe life of the planet, which must be saved from the abusive actions of humans. In other words, the world is not subjected to humans' desire and interest. This is in fact the main message of Ecumenical Patriarch Bartholomew, who has devoted his life to the protection of creation. What we recognize in his statements is the importance of the community over the importance of the individual. The whole is more important than any part of it, including the human part. In other words, humans are *part of nature*, although often they are understood as being *apart from nature*.

In other words, Ecumenical Patriarch Bartholomew advocates that caring for creation must be a Christian concern, which is above and beyond doctrinal differences. All Christians individually and collegially must be stewards of the earth as part of their God-given mission, giving primary place in their life to ecological actions and initiatives.

His pioneering mind has succeeded in mobilizing, environmentally speaking, hundreds of millions of people of the Orthodox Church in at a worldwide level. He has criticized the "culture of over-consumption," and also the "limitless technological development" which has triggered more poverty in the developing countries of the South. Most often, the most vulnerable are the poor who are affected by the pollution of air, land, and water, and whose livelihoods and survival are threatened. Therefore, the poor lands of the South have become the garbage dump of the rich and developed countries of the North. Consequently, it has become clear that "economics is a matter of faith and has an impact on human existence and all of creation."[52]

Moreover, due to eco-theology Ecumenical Patriarch Bartholomew has managed to give a new perspective to Christian mission and a new hermeneutical context to the gospel. He has publicly spoken about the ecological justice and the integrity of creation, about the rights of nature and the obligation of society to protect its own "ecumenical house." "Climate change constitutes a matter of social and economic justice ... there is a close link between the economy of the poor and the warming of our planet," he stated in his 2006 message to the WCC Working Group on Climate Change.[53] Therefore, Christians must be educated spiritually to remain humble in their relationship to the earth, respecting the rules and the rights of nature. According to Patriarch Bartholomew: "Humans are made by God to serve as stewards and priests within the created world."[54] Additionally, he states: "Mais qu'en est-il des droits de la terre—à la quelle nous participons et en dehors de laquelle nous

---

[52] https://www.oikoumene.org/en/resources/documents/central-committee/2009/report-on-public-issues/statement-on-eco-justice-and-ecological-debt.
[53] "Statement for the WCC Working Group on Climate Change," August 2005 (Geneva: WCC, 2006).
[54] *On Earth as in Heaven: Ecological Vision and Initiatives of Ecumenical Patriarch Bartholomew*, ed. John Chryssavgis (New York: Fordham University Press, 2012), 21.

ne pouvons exister? Qui parlera au nom des ressources de notre planète qui sont sans voix ? Qui protégera la diversité silencieuse de ses espèces? Allons-nous accepter la responsabilité de pousser notre environnement vers un point de non-retour?"[55]

On the other side, there are people who emphasize the doctrine of the image of God in humanity in an exclusivist way, rejecting any kind of eco-theological arguments such as the human stewardship of nature. This mindset of stewardship over nature comes in contradiction to many who hold the opinion that justice is applicable only to humans, even if they have obligations to other species. John Rawls, Darrel Moellendorf, and Tim Scanlon are a few among other philosophers who believe that only humans have rights and consequently can be owed justice, since humans are able to enter into a contract, while animals are not able to make claims. Additionally, there is a third perspective held by those who believe that some interests of animals can and should be prioritized over humans' interests. However, they still think that the principle of justice is suitable only for humans' relationships, while animals' rights should be arranged according to the principle of *compassion*.[56]

---

[55] "Soin de la Création, Justice écologique et éthique - Vers la OP21: La société civile mobilisée pour le climat," Réflexions du Patriarche Œcuménique Bartholomée, National Museum of Manille, February 26, 2015, at http://www.ec-patr.org/docdisplay.php?lang=gr&id=2009&tla=gr.

[56] Robin Attfield, "Ecological Justice, Climate Justice and Animals," in Lukas Andrianos, Jan-Willem Sneep, and Guillermo Kerber, eds., Sustainable Alternatives for Poverty Reduction and Eco-Justice, vol. 1 (Chania: Orthodox Academy of Crete, 2013), 65.

Nevertheless, the earth is our common house, where all people, believers and non-believers, live under the same roof, but in separate rooms and unfortunately divided. It seems to my eyes that the earth invites us to overcome the reasons for divisions in order to save the life of the present and of future generations. All Christians must answer that call, by building bridges of dialogue, reconciliation, and mutual acceptance.

Who are we? What is our identity? Where on earth is Jesus after all? Jesus is in our midst as He promised. However, as long as we keep building walls and fences of self-sufficiency, self-righteousness, and idolatry, we shall never succeed in being truly, ontologically, united, due to our inhuman way of treating the earth and our fellow people. In other words, the environmental task unites us, because apart from our common actions, we should learn from scratch to pray together in agreement (*consenserint*) for the protection of the environment. Thus, it is a sign of truthfulness to God each time Christians act and pray together for the well-being of the *oikoumene* and of the whole universe, since the whole creation is groaning and travailing in expectation of salvation. This attitude in fact is the truth of our identity. So, people must struggle for ecological justice serving God. However, this struggle *is not merely against others, but also against our own self-righteous ideals which reinforce collective structures of inhumanity and oppression.*[57]

---

57 Konrad Raiser, "Spirituality of Resistance," in *Passion for Another World: WCC, Internal Encounter of Churches, Agencies and Other Partners on the World Bank and IMF, Geneva 11-12/9/2003* (Geneva: WCC, 2004), 6.

In that framework, the role of the Church's leaders is extremely important, because they are able to guide and influence the faithful members. Political leadership also has an equally important role to play in these matters, since it is up to politicians to decide what measures to implement. Only political will is able to bring justice and enable poor majorities to have a share in the benefits of development and participation in the decision making process. What then is religions' role and how can they contribute to tackling this issue? Religions offer the moral values and the spiritual background for these measures. The initial zeal will soon wear off, unless religions provide society with the appropriate moral justification of the cause.[58]

As mentioned above, the earth is our common house, in which we are called to live together. However, staying together in the same place is not easy to achieve. Therefore, Christians must empty themselves of their personal interests by adopting the *spirituality of communion*. Thus, through communication and cooperation Christians can be led to communion, sharing the same eschatological vision of peace, hope, and love. In other words, protecting the environment is not an option, but an obligation, like a one-way street, where humans must be the voice of the voiceless living species, protecting their diversity and their right to exist.

---

58 Ecumenical Patriarch Bartholomew, *On Earth as in Heaven*, 275.

According to Dr. Father John Chryssavgis,

> Our "heavenliness" should not overshadow our "earthliness." ... We do not have to talk about human beings in exceptionalist or hubristic terms; perhaps our uniqueness or distinction as human beings lies simply in our peculiar relationship to nature. ... We enjoy a binding unity with God's world; it is both helpful and humble for us to recall this truth.[59]

Once again Ecumenical Patriarch Bartholomew in 1997 stated emphatically:

> However, if we do not change within ourselves the attitude of our heart toward our fellow human beings from an attitude of indifference or even enmity to an attitude of friendship, cooperation, and acceptance, then we will achieve nothing in the confrontation of the ecological problems of worldwide interest.[60]

Patriarch Bartholomew claims that humans' concern for the environment should be the outcome of changing society's lifestyle. He states: "The natural environment seems to provide ... a broader, panoramic vision of the world."[61] Accordingly, people should learn to keep unbroken the *environmental covenant* between God, humanity and nature.[62]

---

59 John Chryssavgis, *Creation as Sacrament: Reflections on Ecology and Spirituality* (London: T&T Clark, 2019), 112–113.
60 Ecumenical Patriarch Bartholomew, *On Earth as in Heaven*, 271.
61 Ecumenical Patriarch Bartholomew, *Encountering the Mystery: Understanding Orthodox Christianity Today* (New York: Doubleday, 2008), 89.
62 Rosemary Reuther, "Christianity and Ecology: Seeking the Well-Being of Earth

The ecological crisis is a manifold phenomenon and its roots are cultural, ethical, anthropological and theological. Namely, it is:

- Cultural, because instead of using human creativity and capacities to deepen the meaning of *returning creation to its Creator*, humans have understood themselves as sole creators of this world.
- Ethical, because instead of orienting human action toward a deeper naturalization of humanity and humanization of nature, humans have done the opposite.
- Anthropological, because instead of discovering what it means to be part of nature, humans have set themselves apart from nature.
- Theological, because instead of seeing creation through God's eyes, humans have objectified nature to a point where they no longer experience nature as gift, but as a source for exploitation.[63]

Christian Spirituality and Environment:
From Desacralization to Transfiguration of Creation

It is abundantly true that modern industrialized and economic culture gives value only to "here and now." On the other hand, Bartholomew states that human civilization should stop the

---

and Humans," in D. T. Hessel and Rosemary Ruether, eds., *Eco-Justice at the Center of the Church's Mission* (Cambridge: Harvard University Press, 2000), 603–614.
63 Luca Fiorani, Zsuzsa Román, Valentina Falcioni, and Francesco Geremia, eds., *Proceedings: Relationality between Environmental Awareness and Societal Challenges, Budapest 27–29 May 2016* (Rome: ENEA, 2017), 44.

senseless abuse of natural resources and materials, in which science and technology represent the employment of the human being's intellectual superiority for the purpose of discovering ways to derive the greatest possible profit. Likewise, development has as a leading force and driving power the value of profit, while it seems that the voices of scientists who warn about the dangers of the "greenhouse phenomenon," which threatens the earth's ecosystems, are not taken seriously.

Communities of cities must learn from indigenous communities how to develop a *balanced environmental ethos* as an alternative to the modern urban lifestyle. According to the Ecumenical Patriarch Bartholomew, "Nature is a book, opened wide for all to read and to learn.... When will we learn the alphabet of this divine language?";[64] "We must take the time to listen to the voice of creation. And to do this, we must first be silent."[65] Every living organism, every plant and animal has their own story to unveil. All these forms of life are so different from each other, but at the same time they are interconnected. That beauty of the world can change humans' feelings and the way they treat nature. Having that in mind, people must abandon their arrogant and egoistic manner of abusing creation; instead they must develop a life-code of partnership and cooperation with nature. People's lungs need oxygen to breathe and remain alive. It is clear that humanity cannot survive without nature, since humanity is just a part of the ecosystem. The world

---

64 Ecumenical Patriarch Bartholomew, *Encountering the Mystery*, 91, 92.
65 Ecumenical Patriarch Bartholomew, *Encountering the Mystery*, 90.

is not subjected to humans; instead people are invited to live *in* and *with* nature, which is their natural house (*oikos*). The "Green" Patriarch Bartholomew states again: "The way we relate to material things directly reflects the way we relate to God. The sensitivity with which we handle earthly things clearly mirrors the sacredness that we reserve for heavenly things."[66] Thus, according to Orthodox spirituality, there is a sacred interconnectedness between natural life and the sacramental life of the Church. "If the land is sacred, then our relationship with nature is mystical and sacred too, since in nature God's signs can be traced," claims the Ecumenical Patriarch once again. On the other hand, nature must not be used by theologians as a means of proving God's existence.

Furthermore, according to M. L. Daneel,

> The land is the people, the animals, the plants, and the entire earth community—unborn, living, dead. In other words, the land is the totality of known and unknown existence. Human life can flourish within the context of a community of life. Humans live alongside the soil, water, plants and the other animals.[67]

A new insight was offered by Walter Brueggemann, an Old Testament scholar, who wrote extensively on the so-called "theology of land." God does not give land to people; instead He gives people

---

66 Ecumenical Patriarch Bartholomew, *Encountering the Mystery*, 90.
67 M. L. Daneel, "African Independent Churches Face the Challenge of Environmental Ethics," in *Ecotheology: Voices from South and North*, ed. David G. Hallman (Geneva: WCC, 1994), 248–263.

to land in order to care for it and make it flourish; otherwise God's name is dishonored. This is the paradigm of the Babylonian exile too, where God exiled the people of Israel, so the land could rest from their sins.[68]

According to Rosemary Reuther in her work *Christianity and Ecology*, there are two different theological perspectives which can work complementarily to each other. The first type is called *covenantal*, which originates from the churches with a Protestant biblical background based on the notion of the covenant tradition, and the second type is called *sacramental*, which derives from patristic and medieval mysticism, where the concept of creation is regarded as sacred, as the place where the divine presence is revealed.[69]

To my understanding, the doctrine of "loving your neighbor" must be expanded to "loving your neighborhood," which is more inclusive. The neighbor and nature must be preserved with humility, generosity, and solidarity.[70] This message was in fact delivered by Ecumenical Patriarch Bartholomew: "We must serve our neighbour and preserve our world with both humility and generosity in a perspective of frugality and solidarity alike."[71] Theological institutes,

---

[68] Walter Brueggemann, *The Land: Place as Gift, Promise and Challenge in Biblical Faith* (Minneapolis: Fortress Press, 2002), 138–140.
[69] Ruether, "Christianity and Ecology," 603–614.
[70] See also, David Hallman, *Spiritual Values for Earth Community* (Geneva: WCC, 2000), 33–124.
[71] Ecumenical Patriarch Bartholomew, "Statement for the WCC Working Group on Climate Change," in Lukas Andrianos, Jan-Willem Sneep, and Guillermo Kerber, eds., *Sustainable Alternatives for Poverty Reduction and Eco-Justice*, vol. 1 (Chania:

seminars, and faculties should work together to share information in the field of *eco-theological formation* with ministers, youth, and congregations.

> A Church that neglects to pray for the natural environment is a Church that refuses to offer food and drink to a suffering humanity. At the same time, a society that ignores the mandate to care for all human beings is a society that mistreats the very creation of God, including the natural environment. It is tantamount to blasphemy.[72]

It becomes clear then that Bartholomew's interest in ecology rests also upon the issue of social and economic justice. Ecology is linked with economy, since both try to regulate society's life. He describes that very well in the following passage:

> Specifically, we underscore that the God-wise Fathers of our Church characterize as being righteous or unrighteous those who, respectively, use creation legitimately or absurdly: from the way we make use of creatures are we righteous or unrighteous: says Maximus the Confessor. The use of the world and the enjoyment of material things are shown to be Eucharistic only when they are coupled with praise toward God. If humankind had remained within making normal use of all creatures and "thanking the Creator and all-giving God,"

Orthodox Academy of Crete, 2013), 18.
72 Ecumenical Patriarch Bartholomew, *Encountering the Mystery*, 108.

not only would it not be harmed but also more would be flourishing. ... The problem of the catastrophe of the physical environment is not only a scientific or social one, but also, above all else, an ethical and spiritual one.[73]

For instance, 10% of the global population consumes more than 90% of the natural resources! It seems that humans are trapped in economic, social, and political systems that ignore nature's limits. Consequently, the problems of poverty and unemployment in the wider perspective are also linked with the issue of ecological crisis. In the West after the industrial revolution a civilization of greed developed, which represents humans' preferences and buying habits. Particularly, our modern civilization is marked mainly by human's ego-satisfaction in consumption. Namely, the society of the twenty-first century relies mainly upon unrestricted structural greed, promoting unlimited growth through overconsumption and individualistic behavior.

But what is *greed* and how can we measure and/or control it? In order to answer these questions it is necessary to realize that the issues of poverty, wealth, growth, and environmental crisis are integrally related. Therefore, the WCC developed the program called AGAPE (Alternative Globalization Addressing People and

---

[73] Ecumenical Patriarch Bartholomew, "Patriarchal Greeting," in *Ecothee – Ecological Theology and Environmental Ethics*, ed. Lucas Andrianos, Konstantinos Kenanidis, and Alexandros Papaderos (Chania: Orthodox Academy of Crete, 2009), 1.

Earth), presented at the Ninth General Assembly of the Council in Porto Alegre in 2006. In this process all Christian churches within the WCC focused on how to take measures to eradicate poverty, to challenge accumulation of wealth, and to safeguard ecological integrity. Generally speaking it has been understood that "human greed" is the main danger to the earth's ecosystem within the system of the modern complex economy.

Specifically, *greed* has been defined as the desire to have more than one's share of material goods and power, while other individuals or communities have too few resources to survive, and when the accumulation of wealth and power undermines the common good at the global level.[74] Thus, there are three types of greed: (a) environmental greed / overconsumption of resources, (b) economic greed / monetary accumulation, (c) power greed / social-political inequality.

Ecumenical Patriarch Bartholomew insists that there is an obligation to promote *environmental justice* through the development of *eco-theology* in order to formulate a new ethos and a new lifestyle based on *ecological responsibility*.[75] Therefore, a global and at the same time personal sense of *ecological responsibility* must be developed towards *earthkeeping*. According

---

74 Konrad Raiser, "Theological and Ethical Considerations Regarding Wealth and the Call for Establishing a Greed Line," *Ecumenical Review* 63, no. 3 (October 2011): 278–294.
75 See also, Hans Kung, *Global Responsibility: In Search of a New World Ethic* (New York: Crossroad, 1991), 30.

to professor Ernst Conradie, the notion of *earthkeeping* includes the following points:

- Respect for diverse cultures, species, traditions, etc.
- Sharing the benefits and the responsibility for preserving the common global goods.
- Full participation in decision-making for all who are engaged.
- Solidarity, rebuilding relationships, especially with those who are voiceless and marginalized.
- Sufficiency, not allowing humans' greed to abuse natural resources.[76]

The ecological crisis is not simply a matter of management and technicalities, but it is a matter of changing our spiritual attitude and our worldview. Once people begin to see nature as God's work they realize their own place within nature. Thus, the global community must urgently renew its conception of life and nature, considering the material world as a divine gift, and regaining a *eucharistic spirit* and *an ascetic ethos*.[77] Therefore, the terms *integrity*, *justice*, and *peace* are to be recognized as indispensable dimensions of contemporary Christian ethics. Ecological destruction is a real problem which should be tackled through moral formation of people in combination with praxis. That praxis,

---

76 Ernst Conradie, "The Dispute on Responsible Stewardship as a Metaphor for Christian Earthkeeping," *The South African Baptist Journal of Theology* 16 (2007): 173–190.
77 Ecumenical Patriarch Bartholomew, *Encountering the Mystery*, 100–103.

expressed through prayer, reflection, and transformation, can lead to the transfiguration of all. The fundamental difficulty lies not outside in the ecosystem, but inside us, in the human heart.[78] So, in other words the environmental crisis is absolutely an outward manifestation of the crisis of humanity's mind and heart.

A new eco-theological ethics cannot be developed unless humans realize that they do not exist for their own sake, but for God, and that creation is not a place for them to conquer, but a place which God created for humanity's salvation.[79] In this perspective nature is regarded as the place where God and humans meet each other.[80]

Each one of us is called to make a clear distinction between what we want and what we need. Therefore, societies must adopt a system of a sustainable development, replacing the current one which is based upon greed, accumulation of goods, and endless political ambition. Instead a culture of unselfishness, solidarity, sacrifice, and sharing is urgently needed to replace the culture of consumerism and exploitation, which abuse humans and nature.

---

78 John Chryssavgis and Bruce Foltz, eds., *Toward an Ecology of Transfiguration: Orthodox Christian Perspective on Environment, Nature and Creation* (New York: Fordham University Press, 2013), 88.
79 Kallistos Ware, "Through the Creation to the creator," *Ecotheology* 2 (1997): 8–30.
80 Constantinos Athanasopoulos, "Mystical Ecology: Food and Drink as Spiritual Nourishment in the Mystical Orthodox Tradition," in Lukas Andrianos, Jan-Willem Sneep, and Guillermo Kerber, eds., *Sustainable Alternatives for Poverty Reduction and Eco-Justice*, vol. 1 (Chania: Orthodox Academy of Crete, 2013), 94.

According to the Orthodox understanding the destruction of creation originates from humanity's sin. Nature is the victim of humanity's limitless consumerism and greed, while environmental destruction is equal to suicide, according to Patriarch Bartholomew.[81] Jesus' words are clear: "Take care! Be on your guard against all kinds of greed; for one's life does not consist in the abundance of possessions" (Luke 12:15).

Additionally, the patriarch has declared on many occasions that ecological abuse is not only a sin committed against God, but at the same time it is a crime against humanity, because climate change is an issue of economic, political, and social justice, which affects mostly the young and the future generations, the poorest and the most vulnerable nations and communities around the world.[82] For instance, the low islands of the Pacific, the Great Lakes, the Horn of Africa, the Caribbean, and Southeast Asia are some areas which have been already experiencing the consequences of climate change.

In other words, the whole of creation suffers and groans ("creation has been groaning in labor pains until now," Rom 8:22), because of human inability to set limits to its arrogance. Although the natural world is not itself "fallen" or disobedient to God, Adam's

---

81 Ecumenical Patriarch Bartholomew, *Encountering the Mystery*, 99.
82 Elias Crisostomo Abramides, "HAH Ecumenical Patriarch Bartholomew: The Green Patriarch and His Care for Creation," in Lukas Andrianos, Jan-Willem Sneep, and Guillermo Kerber, eds., *Sustainable Alternatives for Poverty Reduction and Eco-Justice*, vol. 1 (Chania: Orthodox Academy of Crete, 2013), 33.

sin brought the created order into bondage to death, decay, and corruption. Particularly Patriarch Bartholomew stated in 1997:

> To commit a crime against the natural world is a sin. For humans to cause species to become extinct and to destroy the biological diversity of God's creation; for humans to degrade the integrity of the Earth by causing changes in its climate, by stripping the Earth of its natural forests, or destroying its wetlands; for humans to injure other humans with disease; for humans to contaminate the Earth's waters, its land, its air and its life with poisonous substances: these are sins.[83]

The Ecological Contribution of the Encyclical Papal Letter *Laudato Si'*

On June 18, 2015, the publication date of *Laudato Si'*, Pope Francis placed the ecological crisis at the very center of reflection within the Catholic Church. This encyclical became the bridge of communication between Saint Francis of Assisi and another Francis, the pope of Rome. The very famous encyclical letter *Laudato Si'* begins with words taken from the "Canticle of the Creatures" of Saint Francis, praising God by meditating on the goodness of creation as a gift of God.[84] Additionally, Pope Francis established the World Day of Prayer for the Care of Creation (every September

---

83 Ecumenical Patriarch Bartholomew, Address at the Environmental Symposium, Santa Barbara, California, USA, November 8, 1997.
84 https://www.vatican.va/content/dam/francesco/pdf/encyclicals/documents/papa-francesco_20150524_enciclica-laudato-si_en.pdf.

1) for the Catholic Church, in harmony with other Christians. Also, it must be said that after *Laudato Si'* was presented in Rome, on December 13, 2015 in Paris, delegates from 195 countries approved the historic Climate Agreement. As a result of the Paris Agreement, and after twenty-three years and twenty-one conferences, they decided to limit the increase in global mean surface temperature to 2 °C, corresponding to a 1/3 cut in CO_2 emissions. These will reach their peak in 2025 (40 billion tons of CO_2, 36 billion as of today) and will reverse in 2050. From 2021 onward, at least $100 billion per year will be allocated for the transfer of clean technologies from rich countries to poor countries, recognizing a differentiation of responsibility between the former and the latter in causing global warming.

The event which actually gave birth to *Laudato Si'* was a joint workshop under the title "Sustainable Humanity, Sustainable Nature: Our Responsibility" of the Pontifical Academies of Sciences and Social Sciences on May 2–6, 2014. There, the pope of Rome asked the scientists the following question: "What kind of world do we want to leave to those who come after us, to children who are now growing up?" The answer is simple, but not easily implemented: humans should respect the earth as part of God's creation. Therefore, the Bishop of Rome focuses on the relationship between God and humankind through an ecological perspective: the earth must be treated as our common home. "Care for Our Common Home" is also the subtitle of the same encyclical. In other words, this ecologically oriented apostolic letter is actually a spiritual reminder of how people should engage with the earth.

So, the phrase "our planet is our common home" is the key theme of Pope Francis' ecological teaching, but it is also the same one that Ecumenical Patriarch Bartholomew has delivered in his various public messages. The Holy and Great Council of the Orthodox Church states:

> Moreover, we should respect the will of God as manifested through creation. Research must take into account ethical and spiritual principles, as well as Christian precepts. Indeed, due respect must be rendered to all of God's creation in regard to both the way humanity treats and science explores it, in accordance to God's commandment.[85]

Both church leaders, Francis and Bartholomew, have the same pastoral attitude and stand in the same line regarding the ecological issue. They both believe in linking directly and indirectly the destruction and over-exploitation of natural resources with pollution, water scarcity, loss of biodiversity, and global economic inequality. *Climate change is one of the principal challenges facing humanity in our day, while on the other hand human activity through its industrial development, the limitless consumerism and greed are the primary reason of earth's warming phenomenon*, declares the pope of Rome, Francis.

---

[85] Holy and Great Council, *The Mission of the Orthodox Church in Today's World*, §F.12, September 9, 2022, https://www.holycouncil.org/mission-orthodox-church-todays-world.

Laudato Si' describes the need to tackle climate change along with the rapid loss of biodiversity. Therefore, a serious reduction in carbon emissions and other greenhouse gases, the development of renewable energy sources and related storage capacity, and a transition to energy-efficient methods of production and transportation must take place at a worldwide level. For instance, the document recommends a switch from coal and oil to solar and wind power, while at the same time the protection of tropical forests is another area of environmental action.[86]

How beautifully the pope of Rome in his encyclical letter underlines the importance of "communiocentrism," shifting from anthropocentrism and individuality to collectivity. Ecumenical Patriarch Bartholomew points out exactly the same thing, since humans must not be regarded individually over and against nature, but only in relation to the rest of creation. Piero Pasolini used to say something very important: "Everything exists for something else, everything is in relationship. The Gospel revealed to us, that man also advances through relationship. With the principle of mutual love, brought by Jesus, humanity changes, it becomes something else, a new human society."[87] On the contrary, the supporters

---

86 Jos Cardoso Duarte, "Laudato Si' Encyclical: Entropy, Life and Revelation of John," in Louk Andrianos and Tom Sverre Tomren, eds., *Contemporary Ecotheology, Climate Justice and Environmental Stewardship in World Religions* (Latvia: Embla Academisk and Orthodox Academy of Crete, 2021), 140–155.
87 Fiorani et al., eds., *Proceedings: Relationality between Environmental Awareness and Societal Challenges, Budapest 27-29 May 2016*, 16.

of anthropocentrism claim that everything exists for the sake of humanity, and that only humans have moral standing.

Both Francis and Bartholomew claim wisely that the human is not the master of the universe but the steward, the one who offers his service for the benefit and well-being of creation. As long as humans perceive nature as an object they will continue to misunderstand the biblical concept of "dominion" in the book of Genesis as mastery and domination of humankind over nature. However, the original and authentic meaning of dominion is guiding creation toward the Creator in terms of service and stewardship.

Unless society adopts an ecologically oriented lifestyle, the earth's destruction will not stop. In that framework, there must be interaction between natural systems and social systems, since the ecological problem is quite complicated. On the one hand there is a purely environmental crisis, and on the other hand there is a social crisis, because the communities that suffer most from climate change are those of developing and low-income countries. This situation forces many people to abandon their homes due to ecological degradation, becoming *environmental refugees*. So, according to *Laudato Si'*, the richest and most developed countries must substantially assist the poorest and most vulnerable communities in terms of economy, by establishing methods which can lead to a reduction of emissions and by combating poverty and restoring the lost dignity of these indigenous communities.

Therefore, it is necessary that Orthodox and Catholics renew their relationship working together in the field of ecology. A deep and mutual trust must be built between the two Churches upon the care of our common house, which all people (faithful and not faithful) share. It is also important for the two historical Churches to realize soon that besides the doctrinal issues that keep them separated, there is also another path of dialogue that could lead Christianity to an organic and environmental *unity in via*. In this perichoretic scheme of unity, all engaged parties keep their own identity, remaining united without mixture, modification, absorption, or confusion.

In order to understand the above statement, ecology must be seen through the doctrine of creation, in accordance with the anthropological teaching of the Church Fathers, the doctrine of Jesus' incarnation and the sacrament of the Divine Eucharist. For instance, in liturgy people are reconciled and reconnected to each other, to nature, and ultimately to God. So, the mission of the Church is to reconcile the whole world with God; otherwise if we neglect the *missio Dei*, we neglect God's salvation of the world. Furthermore, liturgy offers to community an eschatological perspective. In other words, the Church attempts through liturgy to renovate the current world into a new cosmos.[88]

---

[88] Liz Marsh, "Anamnesis and Restoration in the Eucharist: Towards a Hopeful Liturgical Theology of Climate Change," in in Louk Andrianos and Tom Sverre

Chiara Lubich spoke too about the need for humans to contribute to the earth's transfiguration into an earthly paradise. In liturgy people pray for a new creation, where all participate equally and spiritually. Thus, the *culture of ecological reformation* should convert and renew people's minds in order to rediscover the values which can serve as the foundation for a just life. *Metanoia* (repentance) and *reconciliation* are key points to humanity's transfiguration.[89]

Another paradigm is the Orthodox teaching about the meaning of *ascesis* within modern social life as a solution to the current ecological problem. Ascesis means that people are able to resist consumerism by setting limits to themselves and by saying "Enough, no more materialism in our life." In building such a *spirituality of resistance against the temptation of consumerism (buying new things all the time)*, the notions of *openness, connectedness,* and *earthiness* should be applied at the ecumenical level.

Openness means willingness to make room for the other and to open oneself to the action of the Spirit;

Connectedness means the recognition that life is sustained by bonds of community, where people and earth coexist harmoniously;

Earthiness binds the ecumenical spirituality to the everyday conditions of life at a given time and place.

Tomren, eds., *Contemporary Ecotheology, Climate Justice and Environmental Stewardship in World Religions* (Latvia: Embla Academisk and Orthodox Academy of Crete, 2021), 37–69.

89 Ecumenical Patriarch Bartholomew, Μηνύματα και Ομιλίαι διά το Περιβάλλον [*Messages and Addresses for the Environment*] (Athens: Fanarion, 2002), 341–403.

The Orthodox Church stated in the Holy and Great Council in 2016 in Crete: "Orthodox Tradition, shaped by the experience of Christian truths in practice, is the bearer of spirituality and the ascetic ethos, which must especially be encouraged in our time."[90] In that process of ascesis people learn to sacrifice their own interests for the sake of community, identifying in creation the very energy of God. Hence, *ascesis* and *sharing* are actually two sides of the same coin, reflecting the meaning of eucharistic gathering, where *Jesus is in our midst* and shared by all.[91] This eucharistic attitude of sharing things goes against human greed. Vera Araujo describes that as the "culture of giving," which is actually the first vocation of humankind as "homo donator," whose identity reveals itself in self-giving in all situations and by all means.[92]

Conclusions

According to my understanding, a new "ecological covenant" should be approved and accepted by all communities. It has been proved that both Churches share the same ecological vision and they have the same concerns and worries about the future of the earth. Therefore, the Focolarini members, having the abundant charism of unity provided by God, could be pioneers toward that aim through their project *EcoOne*, along with the Halki Summit

---

90 *The Mission of the Orthodox Church in Today's World*, §F.13.
91 *The Mission of the Orthodox Church in Today's World*, §F.14: "The Church hopes for the recapitulation of everything in the Body of Christ."
92 Vera Araujo, "La cultura del dare," *Nuova Umanità* 125 (1999): 489–510.

conferences which could develop an environmental education program of studies for the young generations.

Furthermore, the prophetic ministry of both church leaders, Pope Francis and Patriarch Bartholomew, is also found in Chiara Lubich's theological mindset. Likewise, Chiara speaks about the recovery of the original relationship between person (human) and nature. Hence, the eschatological present calls people to be united in the one "God-person-nature relationship," in Chiara's words.[93]

Also, there is something in the conference's title which attracted my attention. It's not the importance of the names, or their prophetic ministry, but a small though powerful simple word: "together" (*insieme*). So, no matter what position we hold in the Church, we are together in this world. This is our common vocation and our common call to service toward the ecological crisis. We must understand that there is no Muslim river, Protestant forest, Orthodox sea, or Catholic mountain. We are all one and united in this effort, and either all or none will make it, since the earth is humans' common heritage and unique *oikos*. The earth appeals to Christians for cooperation urgently; even the underground of Constantinople full of remnants of Byzantine churches, along with the catacombs of Rome, proves their common historical roots. Why do we remain distant from each other, while society asks churches to take on common actions, to share common visions, to show common love, and to share the common Jesus? There is need for

---

93 Fiorani et al., eds., *Proceedings: Relationality between Environmental Awareness and Societal Challenges, Budapest 27-29 May 2016*, 42.

tangible environmental engagement deployed at an ecumenical level, necessarily linked with the grassroots of the two sister Churches, inspired and guided by these two great church leaders.

The question I leave you with is the following: Are we brothers and sisters in Christ, or not? I believe we are, indeed. All that we have heard through the conference shows two things: first, we are united in Christ, having the living presence of Jesus among us; and second, that the earth is our common home.

4. TEACHING AND ADVANCING A NEW PARADIGM: EVANGELICAL AND EDUCATIONAL PERSPECTIVES

Vincenzo Zani

I warmly thank the Ecumenical Patriarchate of Constantinople for having promoted, in collaboration with the Sophia University Institute, the Fifth Halki Summit on such an important theme inspired by the prophetic ministry of Pope Francis and Ecumenical Patriarch Bartholomew.

The topics of this conference take on a fundamental character for today's society and for the deep cultural challenges that it faces. Pope Francis and Patriarch Bartholomew, with their magisterium anchored in the gospel message and with great courage, are grappling with the most pressing issues, offering strategic approaches and effective perspectives of an educational nature that are very useful and inspirational, especially for the formation of younger generations.

The purpose of my speech is to illustrate above all the proposal of the "Global Educational Pact," launched by Pope Francis precisely to respond to the change of era that is taking place today. Many initiatives and activities have already been developed around this proposal at various levels and, thanks to events such as this Summit, they can be further promoted, especially at the academic and scientific research level, in the various fields of knowledge.

Why Did Pope Francis Launch the Global Education Pact Proposal?

On September 12, 2019, Pope Francis issued an invitation to an event to be held in Rome in May 2020, aimed at sealing the commitment to implement a *global educational pact* to accompany the formation of the younger generations. It all had to be postponed because of the pandemic, which deeply changed everyone's existence and way of life. Health difficulties have been followed by economic and social ones, and now the consequences of the tragic war situation in Europe are also being added. Educational systems around the world are suffering at both school and academic levels.

The extent of these phenomena is causing a widespread sense of uncertainty that has surprised everyone: individuals and families, peoples, civil society and nations, teachers and educators. As Pope Francis said in that incredible moment of prayer in the square of Saint Peter's Basilica, all of us "Like the disciples in the Gospel we were caught off guard by an unexpected, turbulent storm."[94] In his video message of October 15, 2020, the pontiff relaunched the Educational Pact by placing it in the context of the dramatic pandemic phenomenon and linking it, not only to the encyclical *Laudato Si'*, as he had already done in his previous message, but also to the new encyclical *Fratelli Tutti*, published a few days earlier. He returned to this topic on several occasions, such as in the annual message for the World Day of Peace on January 1, 2021, in the message to the UN on the occasion of the fifth anniversary of COP 25 on climate, and at the COP 26 summit held in Glasgow.

A very significant event was the one held on October 5, 2021 in the Vatican. On the occasion of the World Day of Teachers and Educators, promoted by UNESCO since 1994, the pontiff wanted to meet with representatives of religions on the theme "Religions and education." In addition to the speeches of the leaders present, including Patriarch Bartholomew, a message was delivered to the UNESCO Director addressed to all teachers worldwide, inviting them to work together for an open and inclusive education of each and all.[95]

---

94 Pope Francis, Extraordinary Moment of Prayer on the Square of Saint Peter's Basilica, March 27, 2020.
95 Pope Francis, in his greeting to the representatives of the religions, stressed the importance of uniting efforts for a broad educational alliance to rebuild the fabric of relations for a more fraternal humanity. In one passage he said: "If in the past differences have put us in conflict, today we see in them the richness of different ways to reach God and to educate the new generations to peaceful coexistence in mutual respect" (Address of the Holy Father, Meeting on Religions and Education, Vatican City, October 5, 2021).

II. Theological Perspectives

With these messages, also shared at the ecumenical and interreligious dialogue level, the educational pact takes on an even broader and more concrete framework out of which emerge a line of thought and a strategy that can generate pathways and projects at all levels: educational, scientific, social, and ecclesial. Young people, as the main target audience, are invited to become protagonists of a culture of dialogue and a civilization of harmony.

What Does It Mean to Build a Global Educational Pact?

Pope Francis' proposal summarizes and unifies the long journey of the ecclesial magisterium and social reflection that has unfolded from the Second Vatican Council to today. The global educational pact is a mandate entrusted to adults, educational institutions, and public figures as well as to all religious expressions "to work together to promote, those forward-looking initiatives that can give direction to history and change it for the better."[96] It is therefore necessary to begin processes of transformation without fear to look to the future with hope,[97] by investing in young people.

And to that end, the Council states that, "the education of youth from every social background has to be undertaken, so that there can be produced not only men and women of refined talents, but those great-souled persons who are so desperately required by our

---

96 Cf. Pope Francis, Message for the Launch of the Global Educational Pact, Vatican City, September 12, 2019.
97 Cf. Pope Francis, Message for the Launch of the Global Educational Pact.

times."[98] Everyone has the right to an education that is "in harmony with their fraternal association with other peoples in the fostering of true unity and peace on earth."[99] To this end, all children and young people must be helped, through collaboration between families, educational institutions, and society, to harmoniously develop their capacities to be builders of the common good in a society based on fraternity.

In this regard, Pope Francis appeals to everyone and above all to juridical personalities as well as social, cultural, and political institutions to contribute to the realization of a *new humanism*, which must find its effective application in the various articulations of educational processes on the basis of certain fundamental principles. In numerous messages and speeches addressed to different recipients—educators, religious, bishops, university rectors, diplomatic corps, etc.—the pontiff has highlighted several objectives of the pact that can be summarized in three main headings.

Placing the Person at the Center

If you want to give a soul to formal and informal educational processes, the pope writes,[100] you must have *the courage to place the human person at the center* based on a sound anthropology. And then he adds: "In the development of an integral ecology, a

---

98 Second Vatican Council, Pastoral Constitution *Gaudium et Spes*, §30.
99 Second Vatican Council, Declaration *Gravissimum Educationis*, §1.
100 Pope Francis, Message for the Launch of the Global Educational Pact.

central place must be given to the value proper to each creature in its relationship to the people and realities surrounding it, as well as a lifestyle that rejects the throw-away culture."[101] It is, therefore, a matter of "humanizing education," following in the footsteps of the anthropological choice advocated by the Second Vatican Council, placing itself in dialogue with the parable of modernity. It is such a central and decisive topic that the pope has decided to relaunch it so that it can be explored in all its dimensions and applied in concrete terms, in this era of human history.

On the subject of the centrality of the person, examining the outcomes of modernity, on the one hand, it should be noted that the emphasis placed on subjectivity and self-awareness, which is an undoubted gain of the modern era, cannot ultimately fail to result in the implosion of the subject upon itself (as can be seen in the many outcomes of postmodernity), when it is no longer able to perceive and establish in itself, and from himself as consciousness, the space of the transcendence of God, in God. On the other hand, it should also be noted that when the transcendence of the relationship with God is proposed solely within the horizon of the intersubjective relationship, it is evident that the latter is loaded with such a weight of absoluteness that it becomes destructive either of itself or otherness or of both.[102] It is a matter, then, of taking the *anthropological turn*, through the various expressions of

---

101 Pope Francis, Message for the Launch of the Global Educational Pact.
102 Cf. Piero Coda, *Il Concilio della misericordia sui sentieri del Vaticano II* (Rome: Città Nuova, 2015), 233ff.

personalism, and going deeper into the need for an anthropological paradigm shift, which has its founding root and shaping form in the *originality of the Christian event*. It therefore requires an approach that is first and foremost theological in order to be able to grasp the related philosophical reflection and investigation of the human and natural sciences.[103]

The need to focus on the person—moving from the absolute value of the principle of the person as a pedagogical system to the person understood as a subject open to transcendence (in the sense of the relationship with the Other and with others)—then leads, according to Pope Francis' proposal, to "find other ways, based on a sound anthropology, of envisioning economics, politics, growth and progress."[104]

The centrality of the person, as well as humanizing education, refers to the theme of human rights, that is, the fundamental needs of each person that must be met to ensure an adequate realization of each person in the totality of their material and spiritual dimensions. Human rights find their ultimate source in the dignity of the person and consequently precede written laws, which can only recognize them and not create them. Every person who comes into the world carries within him or her the fundamental rights that must be respected and developed in growth and education.

---

103 Cf. Coda, *Il Concilio della misericordia*, 233ff.
104 Pope Francis, Message for the Launch of the Global Educational Pact.

Promoting a Culture of Dialogue and Inclusion

A second aspect that Pope Francis proposes with the educational pact, *is the courage to capitalize on our best energies, creatively and responsibly.*[105] If, on the one hand, this statement is in line with a large body of literature found in the guidelines of international bodies on the subject, on the other hand, it includes some passages that give this indication a very concrete character. Pope Francis affirms that it is necessary, first of all, to elaborate "a long-term vision unfettered by the status quo"; to prepare "men and women who are open, responsible, prepared to listen, dialogue and reflect with others"; these, then, must be able to "weave relationships with families, between generations, and with civil society, and thus to create a new humanism."

The importance of *dialogue* emerges in this regard. The culture of dialogue is an answer to the problem of differences. What we all have to learn today is to discover that the one who is *different* from us is in truth our *other*. The other is different because it is the external face that looks "towards" me, the face that reveals me to myself as I too am a face capable of encounter. Therefore, this second passage indicated by the pope also offers considerable food for thought at a pedagogical level, but first of all at a psychological and social level. The first step in building dialogue is to listen. As the pontiff says, we must listen to everyone's voice and, in particular, to

---

105   Pope Francis, Message for the Launch of the Global Educational Pact.

those of children, teenagers, and young people, passing on values and knowledge, to build a future of justice and peace together.

The emphasis on a culture of dialogue involves not only the community of believers but must become a commitment for the whole of humanity. From this perspective, identity and difference, also in the educational field, are not opposing terms, but articulations of an *anthropology*, in which self-esteem and the care of the other constitute the interdependent poles of the *sense of responsibility*. It is on these two dimensions that it is possible to base a prosocial-altruistic education, which combines the ability to decentralize and help others with an adequate sense of self-worth.[106]

Rethinking the educational-didactic pathway, in this perspective outlined by the educational pact, and more generally, reviewing "knowledge" in terms of relationship and otherness requires a commitment to go beyond a simple methodological organization to implement a true *anthropological re-founding*, which extends to the totality of the educational event.[107] Taking on this perspective means, then, assigning the *diversity* dimension the same importance that is rightly given to that of *identity*, an indispensable reference point for the development of the self, but insufficient if not considered in the line of openness and dialogue with plurality. Only in this way, by reestablishing a *pedagogy of otherness*, will it be

---

106 Cf. Michele De Beni, *Educare all'altruismo* (Trento: Erikson, 2000), 29.
107 Cf. Antonio Nanni, "Ripensare l'educazione a partire dall'altro," in Giuseppe Lupo, ed., *Educare all'altro nella scuola* (Leumann [Turin]: Elle Di Ci, 1994), 147–168.

possible to overcome fear or mistrust of all diversity (of age, culture, religious affiliation, philosophy of human and social development) and to develop attitudes of discussion, research, and acceptance,[108] which underpin the culture of dialogue and inclusion.

Serving Future-Oriented Development

The third directive pointed out by the pope is the *courage to train individuals who are ready to offer themselves in service to the community.*[109]

One can read in this orientation the invitation to form active protagonists of the common good to globalize solidarity and hope and build a world of peace. Service, which the pope describes by citing the example of Jesus who bent down to wash the feet of the apostles, becomes a criterion by which to measure the methods and the effectiveness of educational projects carried out by various institutions, in particular by Catholic ones.

Why should we make ourselves available for service? To fully understand this third directive, which the pontiff considers as one of the priority paths of the educational pact aimed at building a "village of education," we need to refer to the text of *Gaudium et Spes*, where we can see that the idea of community does not refer

---

108 Education, in the different "places" where it occurs (family, school, associations, etc.), must appropriate the fundamental task of "making people meet," teaching how to use thought, word, action within and in favor of the dimension of encounter, of authentic dialogue. Cf. Giuseppe Milan, *Educare all'incontro: La pedagogia di Martin Buber* (Rome: Città Nuova, 1994), 30ff.

109 Cf. Pope Francis, Message for the Launch of the Global Educational Pact.

to a limited reality, but can be assimilated to that of the whole of humanity. In this context, the Council refers to the concept of the *"world" seen as the "the theatre of man's history,"* which is *the heir of his energies, his tragedies, and his triumphs*.[110] Therefore, the community to be built and served is understood in a local sense and in a universal sense, and stands together if there is solidarity and cooperation.

The proposal for an educational pact therefore refers back to the social magisterium with which the Church addresses itself first and foremost to believers, but also to the whole of humanity on the move and strives to look to the future, to think about the development of humanity in the third millennium in order to improve its living conditions. In this sense, the social encyclicals, up to the most recent *Laudato Si'* and *Fratelli Tutti*, certainly consider the world in its cosmological dimension (i.e. the world as "nature"), but at the same time they have in mind the different and multiple levels of meaning of the concept of humanity–world for which the believer is asked above all for a concrete and active commitment, that is, a generous and supportive service. The educational pact relaunches service in this perspective.

These considerations explain why the pope insists on a commitment to serve the human community, through education.[111]

---

110   Cf. Second Vatican Council, Pastoral Constitution *Gaudium et Spes*, §2b.
111   "Solidarity is certainly expressed in service, which can take very different forms in the way of taking care of others. The service is largely to take care of the fragilities ... of those who are fragile in our families, in our society, in our people." Pope Francis, Encyclical Letter *Fratelli Tutti*, October 3, 2020.

Service is a principle that generates *solidarity*, a sense of the *common good*, the value of *human development*, and the culture of *hope*. That is why it is essential to create a spirit and *style of cooperation*, locally, nationally, and internationally, at school, academic, scientific, and socio-economic levels, in formal and informal pathways, to welcome and respond to the cry that rises from those portions of humanity that suffer from the lack of education, and of means suitable for the development of a solidarity-based humanism, of possibilities for a healthy socialization.

In Conclusion

In the contents of the educational pact, other important interventions of the magisterium of Pope Francis converge, which have been mentioned several times in his messages. These include the Apostolic Exhortation *Evangelii Gaudium*, the Encyclical Letters *Laudato Si'* and *Fratelli Tutti*, and in particular the *Document on Universal Brotherhood* signed on February 4, 2019 in Abu Dhabi with the Grand Imam of al-Azhar, al-Tayyeb.

Taking into consideration the various objectives outlined by the pontiff, the Congregation for Catholic Education has prepared a number of resources (a *handbook* and *guidelines*). The aim is to facilitate their implementation. That is why they have chosen to concentrate on five main areas on which work will focus over the next few years, entrusted to universities, schools, and all other entities that wish to join the project. The topic areas chosen at the global level are as follows: 1. *Dignity and human rights*; 2. *Fraternity and cooperation*; 3. *Technologies and integral ecology*; 4. *Peace and citizenship*; 5. *Cultures and religions*.

The Sophia University Institute will focus on the area of "Cultures and religions," in collaboration with Saint Thomas University in Manila. The change of era, repeatedly recalled by the pontiff, is today further conditioned, accelerated, and made more complex, not only by the pandemic, but also by the war in Ukraine that undermines the heart of Europe and of the entire world.

The scholar Edgar Morin wrote:

> In History the unexpected happens and will repeat itself. We thought we were living certainties, statistics, forecasts and with the idea that everything was stable, whereas everything goes into crisis. We did not realise this. We must learn to live with uncertainty, that is, to have the courage to … resist negative forces.[112]

The global educational pact, aimed at building the "village of education," that is, a cohesive and collaborative humanity, is a particularly suitable and useful tool to live courageously in this age of uncertainty to build the future. The leaders of tomorrow, today's boys and girls, must be helped to acquire values, responsibility, a sense of community, and an awareness of their own role.

---

112 Quoted by Giovanni Lo Storto, "Una bussola di valori per il futuro [A Compass of Values for the Future]," *Corriere della Sera* (April 23, 2022), 36.

III. ETHICAL, LEGAL, AND ECUMENICAL PERSPECTIVES

5. ECOLOGICAL SIN: ETHICS, ECONOMICS, AND SOCIAL REPENTANCE

Chris Durante

Ecological Sin and Our Civilizational Ethos

Ecumenical Patriarch Bartholomew of Constantinople of the Eastern Orthodox Christian ecumene has been a longstanding advocate for the development of an ecological consciousness among both Orthodox Christians and the people of the world at large. Consequently, this essay seeks to make a contribution to the development of the applied dimensions of Orthodox Christian approaches to ecological ethics, as well as demonstrate the ways in which Orthodox Christian ideas, values, and practices may serve as a source of ecological wisdom for all people—even those who do not practice the Orthodox Christian faith.[113]

---

113 Originally published as: "Ecological Sin: Ethics, Economics, and Social Repentance," *Journal of Orthodox Christian Studies* 3, no. 2 (2020): 195–214. © 2020 Johns Hopkins University Press. Reprinted with permission of Johns Hopkins University Press.

One of Patriarch Bartholomew's most salient contributions to ecological ethics has been his usage of the idea of "sin" to refer to the immorality of ecological harms, such as: pollution, climate change, deforestation, and species extinction. Patriarch Bartholomew introduced the concept of "ecological sin" to the world during a speech in Santa Barbara, California in 1997 when he proclaimed,

> For humans to cause species to become extinct and to destroy the biological diversity of God's creation ... For humans to degrade the integrity of Earth by causing changes in its climate, by stripping the Earth of its natural forests, or destroying its wetlands ... For humans to injure other humans with disease, for humans to contaminate the Earth's waters, its land, its air, and its life, with poisonous substances ... These are sins.[114]

In Greek, the word for "sin" is *amartia*, which literally means to "miss the mark." Sin as *amartia* makes sense within the framework of a teleological ethics, and means to fall short of attaining our

---

Although I will at times reference and/or draw upon ideas from non-Orthodox environmental and ecological thought, the primary purpose of this essay is not to place Orthodox Christianity in dialogue with either non-Orthodox approaches to ecological theology or secular environmental ethical and social theories. Rather, by focusing primarily upon Orthodox Christian sources, the aim of this essay is to further develop the idea of "ecological sin" as well as demonstrate ways in which insights from the Orthodox Christian tradition may help foster an ecological consciousness amongst all peoples of goodwill and help enable the global human community—including Orthodox Christians—to ameliorate the ecological crisis we are currently experiencing.

114 Ecumenical Patriarch Bartholomew, Address at the Environmental Symposium, Santa Barbara, California, USA, November 8, 1997.

personal and communal goals of becoming virtuous persons striving to live the good life within excellent communities as we pursue closeness and union with the divine. In other words, the concept of sinning does not necessarily imply a breach of law but also speaks to the goals we pursue, the mindset we adopt, and the type of ethos we foster as persons and communities; all of which influence the ways we relate to one another, the natural world, and the divine.

More recently in 2015, Patriarch Bartholomew spoke of "the need to broaden our narrow and individualistic concept of sin."[115] Patriarch Bartholomew's comment calls attention to the fact that it is not only individuals but also collectives that are capable of sin. When a group of individual persons acts in tandem they can bear shared responsibility for the actions they perform and hence, there exists a moral dimension to group agency. Although collectives do not possess a psyche in the way individual persons do, we often recognize the phenomena of group agency and communal identity and speak of notions such as "collective worldview" and "civilizational ethos" to refer to the ways in which collectives think and act as a single force. When an entire civilization abides by a shared value system and engages in shared behavioral patterns that result in common dispositions, habits, and lifestyles, we may refer to this as a *civilizational ethos*. A civilizational ethos guides a

---

[115] Ecumenical Patriarch Bartholomew, "Ecology, Economy and Ecumenicism," TIME magazine, June 18, 2015. This article appeared amidst the convening of the Paris Climate Accord and the issuing of Pope Francis' encyclical *Laudato Si'*.

general and pervasive way of life and directs patterns of individual and collective behavior by providing us with a conception of ourselves, our world, and our purpose within it. When "sin" is understood as *amartia*, collective sin is to fall short of achieving our personal and communal goals of striving to be virtuous members of a good society pursuing closeness with the divine. Our collective failure to correctly relate to the natural world has been the result of our civilization's misperception of humanity's relationship with creation, which is a direct result of misinterpreting who we are as creatures. As the Orthodox theologian Philip Sherrard has claimed,

> It [the ecological crisis] is not first of all a crisis concerning our environment. It is first of all a crisis concerning the way we think. We are treating our planet in an inhuman, god-forsaken manner because we see things in an inhuman, god-forsaken way.[116]

Sherrard laments the fact that as a global civilization we have adopted a way of thinking in which we no longer recognize the natural world as divinely created, and all that such a vision entails. Sherrard describes the Orthodox understanding of the world as "a sacred cosmology—one that affirms both a sacred human image and a sacred world image"[117] and argues that "the creation

---

116 Philip Sherrard, "Human Image, World Image: The Renewal of Sacred Cosmology," in *Toward an Ecology of Transfiguration: Orthodox Christian Perspective on Environment, Nature and Creation* (New York: Fordham University Press, 2013), 211.
117 Sherrard, "Human Image, World Image," 219.

of the world is ... the expression of divine life."[118] As the Orthodox theologian John Zizioulas explains, "The Christian regards the world as sacred because it stands in dialectical relationship with God."[119] It is through this relationship that ecological life, and the biosphere itself, begets its vitality to create and sustain life—including our own.

During the past few centuries humanity, throughout the industrialized and industrializing world,[120] has adopted a self-understanding in which we tend to overemphasize our self-determinative capacities and view ourselves as "masters over nature," and hence, we have developed a tendency to view the natural world solely in terms of its value as a utility to be exploited for human pleasure or profit.[121] To adhere to a mindset, and uphold a worldview, in which nature is objectified and valued solely for

---

118   Sherrard, "Human Image, World Image," 219.
119   John Zizioulas, "Priests of Creation," in *Environmental Stewardship*, ed. R. J. Berry (New York: T& T Clark International, 2006), 289–290. Orthodox Christian theology may be described as panentheistic, meaning a belief that the divine permeates all of creation, including all forms of biotic and abiotic existence in the cosmos. Unlike "pantheism," which means "all is divine," the term "panentheism" means "all is in the divine," and hence, that the divine is the "ground-of-being," so to speak, or "that-from-which-all-that-exists-begets-its-existence." This implies that although natural creation ought to be treated with the utmost respect, it is not to be worshiped. Unlike other forms of Christian panentheism, namely the views of process theologians such as John Cobb—whom I cite in this article—the Orthodox Christian form of panentheism maintains that there is no way in which the divine may be affected or altered by creation.
120   Especially in the "Western world" but also in any advanced industrialized society, such as China, for example.
121   Michael Northcott, *The Environment and Christian Ethics* (Cambridge, UK: Cambridge University Press, 1996), 40–42.

the satisfaction of humankind's desires for pleasure or profit is to misconstrue the importance of respecting natural creation; to misunderstand what it means for our species to flourish; and to fail to realize how intimately connected the well-being of our natural world is with our own. By upholding distorted value-hierarchies, false ideals, and skewed goals, our civilizational ethos has been capable of creating a communal way of life and collective patterns of behavior that continually and perpetually miss the mark when it comes to living in proper relation with the natural world. Our ecological sins are a result of our failure to respect nature as an expression of divine life and our failure to see ourselves as integral members of creation rather than as masters of an alien environment. In order to stop committing our ecological sins, we must recognize the robust nature of what it means to exist as human beings in relation to the world and strive to live in right relationship with the entire web of existence of which we are a part. We are capable of participating in the perpetual processes of regeneration that sustain the vitality of our world and as such, may view relating to nature regeneratively as a means of growing closer with the vital divine energies sustaining life on our planet.

In the aforementioned speech in 1997, Patriarch Bartholomew claimed:

> As individuals, we live not only in vertical relationships to God, and horizontal relationships to one another, but also in a complex web of relationships that extend throughout our

lives, our cultures and the material world. Human beings and the environment form a seamless garment of existence; a complex fabric that we believe is fashioned by God.[122]

Explaining how, from the Orthodox Christian perspective, nature is believed to be "fashioned by God," as well as highlighting the immense moral responsibility that follows from such a view, the Orthodox theologian Nikos Nissiotis states:

> Nature, regarded as creation, *ktisis,* is presented in Scripture as an organism undergoing renewal. This is a consequence of the basic thesis that all things have been created through the Word of God, and hence all things are subject to His work of renewal through the Holy Spirit. ... Creation in this case, that is nature as matter, is presented as a living organism that develops and is renewed together with man through his genuine re-creative cooperation in the creative work of God. The moral responsibility that stems from the above notion of renewal and the obligation under which it places everyone ... is enormous, because by their work they participate in God's work or renewal, when this is understood in all its breadth and not in the context of a narrow individual morality.[123]

---

122   Ecumenical Patriarch Bartholomew, Address at the Environmental Symposium, Santa Barbara, California, USA, November 8, 1997.
123   Nikos Nissiotis, "Nature and Creation: A Comment of the Environmental Problem from a Philosophical and Theological Standpoint," in *Toward an Ecology of Transfiguration: Orthodox Christian Perspective on Environment, Nature and Creation* (New York: Fordham University Press, 2013), 201.

If, as Nissiotis claims, we, as the *human community*, have a *moral responsibility* to engage in re-creative cooperation with the natural world as a means of partaking in the divine work of *perpetual renewal of life*, then this implies that when humans disregard the earth and engage in ecologically harmful and destructive practices, they are not only failing to respect God by failing to respect His creation but are being negligent of their moral responsibility of entering into a life-bestowing relationship with creation.[124] Hence, we must cultivate an authentic care for our biospheric creation in all of its biodiversity for it is our *oikos*, or home, as well as our system of life support and kindred being. As Nissiotis says,

> We do not protect the environment because it is beautiful and useful but because it is material that belongs to creation, because it is a creative organism, something forever unique, and because we identify ourselves with a profound material and spiritual-ethical relationship leading to a right coexistence and cooperation.[125]

Collective Sin, Economics, and Moral Responsibility

Patriarch Bartholomew has argued that "[t]he root cause of our environmental sin lies in our self-centeredness and in the mistaken order of values, which we inherit and accept without any critical evaluation."[126] Arguably, the root cause of our ecological sinfulness

---

[124] Willis Jenkins, *Ecologies of Grace: Environmental Ethics and Christian Theology* (New York: Oxford University Press, 2008)

[125] Nissiotis, "Nature and Creation," 202.

[126] Ecumenical Patriarch Bartholomew, Message at the International Conference on Ethics, Religion, and Environment, University of Oregon, April 5, 2009.

is our personal and civilizational egoism as human beings, or anthropocentrism, and our disordered value system, as well as our personal and communal failure to critically reevaluate and revise our ways of living and the principles that inform them. This is in large part because our contemporary civilizational ethos has been permeated by an economic understanding of the person and of well-being, which aims for perpetual material and financial growth at the expense of ethical and psycho-spiritual maturation. As a result we often pursue immediate pleasures rather than long-term benefits and have allowed ourselves to be governed by the vices of avarice, in the guise of economic growth, and gluttony, in the guise of maximal consumption and enrichment.

The neoclassical paradigm of economics that now dominates global society in its neoliberal manifestation ultimately aims for the goal of perpetual profit via perpetual expansion and functions according to a utilitarian mindset that seeks to commodify both an array of living beings as well as all forms of creative human activity.[127] It posits a view of the human person as an intrinsically self-interested and rationalistic individual seeking to maximize her own benefits and satiate her own desires, at almost any cost.[128]

---

127 Herman Daly and John Cobb, Jr., *For the Common Good: Redirecting the Economy toward Community, the Environment and a Sustainable Future*, 2nd ed. (Boston: Beacon Press, 1994), 87; Herman Daly, "Economics for a Full World," Great Transition Initiative (June 2015).

128 Daly and Cobb, *For the Common Good*, 159; Sallie McFague, *Life Abundant: Rethinking Theology and Economy for a Planet in Peril* (Minneapolis: Fortress Press, 2001), 81; Sallie McFague, *A New Climate for Theology: God, the World, and Global Warming* (Minneapolis: Fortress Press, 2008), 83.

As such, this dominant socio-economic paradigm envisions the natural world as being replete with interchangeable resources for consumption and manipulation, with the ultimate goal of social life as the competitive maximization and accrual of individual capital and wealth, which is to be used for the satiation of unmitigated desire. These elements of the neoclassical/neoliberal paradigm of socio-economic thought stand in stark contradiction to the relational view of personhood, the view of the natural world as creation and kindred being, and communal life as striving for excellence in a state of mutual well-being that are to be found within the Orthodox Christian theological tradition. As Patriarch Bartholomew has claimed,

> The highest pursuit of humanity is not economic enrichment or economic expansion. ... We cannot live by economic development alone, but we must seek ... the values and principles that transcend economic concerns. Once we accept this, the economy becomes a servant of humanity, not its master.[129]

The ethos of neoclassical economics has become so ingrained in our psyches over the course of the past few generations—especially with the emergence of the neoliberal ideology of the late 1970s and early 1980s[130]—that for most people today, the values of this

---

129 Ecumenical Patriarch Bartholomew, Address at Davos Annual Meeting of the World Economic Forum, 1999: Orthodoxy Today.
130 Too often we want to believe that all of our actions, or the actions of our recent ancestors, are and were, good and noble because of the psychological

economic paradigm are predominant in governing their social lives and molding their daily lifestyles.[131] By accepting the parameters of a preexisting civilizational ethos into which they were born, and attempting to function successfully within it, human individuals and communities often fail to truly reflect upon what it means to be good and to pursue authentic flourishing as they become ever more compliant with their civilization's flaws. The environmental philosopher Philip Cafaro notes,

> Public opinion polls repeatedly have shown that most Americans self-identify as "environmentalist" and support strong policies to protect the environment. Yet these same people routinely behave in environmentally irresponsible ways. ... Our poor environmental behavior stems, in part, from particular character defects or vices. Among the most important of these are gluttony, arrogance, greed, and apathy.[132]

The vices, as Cafaro speaks of them, may be thought of as sin habituated and embodied in one's behavior. Sinning can occur as both particular actions and more general patterns of living. For instance, to act greedily is to miss the mark of goodness in a specific situation, whereas to allow greed to habitually motivate our choices

---

satisfaction and contentment it gives us. We must come to understand that we can continue to love our ancestors even after we have realized that they have sinned.
131 McFague, *Life Abundant*, 84; Philip Cafaro, "Taming Growth and Articulating a Sustainable Future: The Way Forward for Environmental Ethics," *Ethics & the Environment* 16, no. 1 (2011): 10.
132 Philip Cafaro, "Gluttony, Arrogance, Greed, and Apathy: An Exploration of Environmental Vice," in *Environmental Virtue Ethics*, ed. Ronald Sandler and Philip Cafaro (New York: Rowan & Littlefield Publishers, 2005), 135.

and behaviors is to allow it to become embodied in our mode of living. When vicious ideals are habituated to the extent that they serve as values upon which we make judgements and through which we discern how to behave, we find ourselves pursuing a sinful life.

In the Orthodox Christian tradition it is believed that we are all sinners and that we may commit sin both voluntarily and involuntarily.[133] These types of sin are grounded in the Aristotelian[134] categories of action in which involuntariness is the result of either coercive force or ignorance. Because most of our behavior, sinful or otherwise, is not performed under the duress of completely coercive force or total ignorance, few of our actions ever performed could be said to be completely involuntary. Many involuntary sins, in the way the concept has traditionally been understood in Orthodox theology, are what we might refer to as mixed actions: an action which is partly involuntary and partly voluntary or, in other words, an action that an agent does indeed cause, yet does so while ignorant of a number of the particular factors and aspects associated with either the circumstances, consequences, or nature of the action itself. In short, most *"involuntary sins" involve an immoral action committed without knowledge of the particulars of the circumstances nor an*

---

[133] John of Damascus, *The Fountain of Knowledge*, Chapter 24: "On Voluntary and Involuntary," in *Saint John of Damascus Writings*, trans. Frederic H. Chase, Jr. (New York: Fathers of the Church, 1958), pp. 253–255.

[134] Aristotle, *Nicomachean Ethics*, Book III:1–5, Book V:8–9, and Book VII:5–10, trans. Terence Irwin (Indianapolis, IN: Hackett Publishing Co., 1999).

accurate understanding of the consequences of one's particular actions and is performed without malice.

In the context of ecological ethics, an example would be if, at an early point in the twentieth century, an individual or group did not yet realize the harmful effects that burning petroleum or the use of DDT and pesticides had on the environment and human life, and they happily continued to do so without making any attempts to either reduce their use of, or cease to use, petrol or pesticides. Despite their lack of awareness of the ramifications of their actions, the extraction of petroleum and its use in automotive transport, and the creation and overuse of synthetic pesticides, still disrupted humanity's relation with the natural world and still caused harm to themselves, the ecosystems, and the atmosphere. Despite having their moral culpability mitigated by the circumstances of their ignorance, this group remains causally responsible for the damaging effects produced by their actions and hence, have inadvertently missed the mark of living in a cooperative and re-creative way with nature; they have involuntarily committed sin out of ignorance.

Beyond an analysis of consequences, we must also ask, what was their primary motivation? If the goal that propelled them toward such activities may be said to have had the common good in mind, such as the use of DDT to prevent malaria and other diseases or to protect crops and thereby food supplies, then their moral culpability is significantly reduced, so long as they changed their ways (or engaged in personal and social repentance) once they discovered the harmful consequences of their actions; as we did with the use of DDT, for instance. If however, a group was motivated by selfish reasons, such as oil extraction and refinement for the sole aims of personal profits and social power, then despite their ignorance of the consequences they may be held morally accountable to a higher degree than the previously imagined group, due to the fact that their primary intent was not aimed at the common good. In regards to the social practices we inherit, we must remain vigilantly attentive to both their intended goals as well as the actual outcomes prior to adopting them. If we become aware that it is not only our inherited practices but also the values underlying them that are missing the mark of goodness, then it is incumbent upon us to critically reevaluate and reform these values and practices.

Unlike our predecessors from the aforementioned example, in our current era, we are all well aware of the ecological crisis and, as such, have a responsibility to seek sound understanding of the circumstances, as well as act in ways that not only avoid ecologically harmful consequences but which seek to repair and restore our broken relationship with the natural world. If part of being virtuous and leading the good life is attempting to live in a re-creative and cooperative manner with ecological systems in that they comprise our biospheric *oikos* and are kindred with us as divinely created being, then our *individualistic, competitive, and growth-oriented economic system has indeed been vicious rather than virtuous.*

Especially in its current neoliberal manifestation, the neoclassical economic system has propelled us to align all aspects of our life with this reductionistic, avaricious, and gluttonous paradigm of thought. To this end, humanity is not only failing to achieve the goal of *being good*, which given humankind's fallibility is expected, but human civilization seems to be aiming for a goal utterly unaligned with an authentic conception of the good and a view of humanity's *telos* that includes re-creative cooperation with the natural world.[135]

Our civilizational ecological sin is perpetuated as a result of a pervasively shared attitude amongst persons whereby moral responsibility for societal vices and social problems is persistently shifted away from themselves, either as individual persons or as smaller local communities, toward larger more abstract and indeterminate entities, such as "the state," "the society," "the corporations," as if persons and communities were not themselves part and parcel of the constitution of these entities. This is the result of a distorted understanding of our moral responsibilities. Responsibility is both our ability to respond to circumstances and other beings, as well as our culpability for our actions and behaviors. When individual persons think and act in tandem with groups,

---

135 While all persons of goodwill seeking to contribute to the common good ought to take heed of our collective teleological misdirection and recognize the centrality that engaging in re-creative cooperation with the natural world plays in cultivating the flourishing of humanity and sustaining life's existence as we know it, from the Orthodox Christian point of view such re-creative cooperation is understood as a means of partaking in the energies of the divine, and therefore engaging in and promoting ecologically regenerative behavior should be seen as not only ethically imperative but also as carrying a spiritual importance as well.

they tend to feel as though their responsibility is diminished, and the danger in this lies in the fact that this sort of thinking can lead one to perceive her individual actions as either insignificant or her personal agency as unable to effectively initiate any sort of redirection of the course of actions being pursued on a collective societal level.

This has resulted in a redirection of our collective attention away from the good and the pursuit of personal and communal excellence and virtue, toward our individual obligations to other individuals and collectives with a view toward what they owe us and what we owe them. A deeply problematic aspect of this limited business-minded view of duty-focused moral responsibility is the reorientation of moral life away from a focus on communal or civilizational virtue and flourishing toward an ethics of calculated exchanges of obligations amongst particular individuals or proximally immediate groups. As a result we often neglect our relationships to ecosystems, the biosphere, the global human community, and future generations, because it is difficult to calculate what we owe them and how we ought to fulfill any such obligation. This is where the relational and virtue oriented approach to ethics can enable us to move beyond a system of obligatory exchange to one in which we truly attempt to understand what genuine flourishing is and how me might go about pursuing it.

To be complicit—without regret—in a system governed by a worldview that fails to recognize the intrinsic value of natural living beings and ecosystems is to be acquiescent to a system of collective behavior that inherently misses the goal of goodness. One who possesses awareness of a social ill being performed by a group and acquiesces to, or passively goes along with, a vicious set of behaviors without protest, acts in a manner that is voluntary insofar as she is a person who intentionally and deliberately performs the action. To knowingly engage in ecologically harmful patterns of behavior and intentionally pursue goals motivated by vicious ideals is to voluntarily engage in sin. Ultimately, *acquiescence to the status quo of a paradigm whose goals do not align with the pursuit of the good is itself a sin*. Rather than acting in ways that attempt to ethically improve our civilization, humanity has transformed our recognition of our own human imperfection from an impetus for striving to be excellent, into a complacent acceptance of imperfection that breeds a defeatist attitude in which moral excellence is neither valued nor sought. When we, individually and collectively, no longer even attempt to pursue moral excellence as our goal, we will inevitably miss the mark of goodness and fall into sin. We must truly come to a point at which we recognize that our collective ecological sin occurs not only when either an individual or a group acts as a single agent[136] but when we—as individuals and smaller communities—adopt, endorse, support, or acquiesce to a dominant civilizational

---

136 For example, when a particular corporation engages in the act of fracking and pollutes the groundwater, harming the health of the humans and nature in a given area.

ethos and economic system that embodies values, goals, and ideals that are at inherently odds with the good.

The ways in which global human civilization has been committing ecological sin speaks to our individual actions, collective patterns of behavior, and the shared paradigms of thought that guide our behaviors. In short, ecological sin is primarily a form of collective sin rooted in our flawed civilizational ethos, which gives rise to the systemic vices that have resulted in our current global environmental crisis. To this end, Patriarch Bartholomew has claimed: "We need a new way of thinking about our own selves, about our relationship with the world and with God. Without this revolutionary 'change of mind,' all our conservation projects, however well intentioned, will remain ultimately ineffective."[137]

Ecological Metanoia and Social Askesis

Global civilization must come to recognize that the economic system to which we all adhere perpetuates the vices of gluttony and avarice, and that by abiding by its models and values we are causing ecosystems to fail and harming the health of the humans who live within them. We must come to realize that without amending our civilizational ethos and to carry on with business as

---

[137] Ecumenical Patriarch Bartholomew, Message at the International Conference on Ethics, Religion, and Environment, University of Oregon, April 5, 2009.

usual without altering our economic models is to perpetuate one of the primary sources of our collective ecological sin: our overly narrow view of human flourishing that has led to the ways in which humanity has missed the mark in terms of living sustainably within our living biospheric home, or *oikos*. This is where, I believe, the Orthodox Christian ethico-spiritual paradigm possesses values and insights from which the global community can benefit, and which may be used to support a more ecological approach to ordering our economic systems and daily lifestyles, regardless of one's religious affiliations or lack thereof. With such recognition, humanity may begin to sincerely repent of its ecological sins by engaging in ways of living and developing new economic models guided by an authentic care for our biospheric home, a recognition of our ecological relatedness with other beings, and a sincere concern for the state of the environment that our future progeny will inherit from us. As with any authentic repentance (*metanoia*), an *ecological metanoia* entails a transformation of each individual's personal lifestyle as well as a transformation of humanity's communal and civilizational ethos, in a manner that has the power to re-create and reform the social world we have constructed and inhabit. Patriarch Bartholomew has claimed that without an authentic repentance that entails a holistic transformation of our mindsets, value hierarchies, and ways of living, we will never be able to effectively put an end to the sins we are committing against the natural environment. He writes:

> We are convinced that the root cause of all our difficulties consists in human selfishness and human sin. What is asked of us is not greater technological skill but deeper repentance, metanoia, in the literal sense of the Greek word, which signifies fervent "change of mind" and radical transformation of lifestyle.[138]

In the Orthodox Christian tradition, engaging in *asceticism*, or the practice of psycho-somatic exercises, serves as a means of entering into repentance so that we may transfigure our dispositions, mindsets and ways of life in a genuine *metanoia*. While asceticism is often associated with eremitic and monastic practices in which practitioners exit society and live in isolation, Patriarch Bartholomew reminds us that this is not the only way of practicing asceticism. He writes,

> Asceticism is not a flight from society and the world, but a communal attitude of mind and way of life that leads to the respectful use, and not the abuse of material goods. Excessive consumption may be understood to issue from a world-view of estrangement from self, from land, from life, and from God. Consuming the fruits of the earth unrestrained, we become consumed ourselves, by avarice and greed. Excessive consumption leaves us emptied, out-of-touch with

---

[138] Ecumenical Patriarch Bartholomew, Message at the International Conference on Ethics, Religion, and Environment, University of Oregon, April 5, 2009.

our deepest self. Asceticism is a corrective practice, a vision of repentance.[139]

A crucial aspect of our daily behavior that is contributing to our environmental destruction and which ties together the economical and the ecological dimensions of our lives is humanity's current consumption habits on individual, collective, and civilizational levels.[140] With a rich tradition of fasting, Orthodox Christianity has held a deep recognition of the ways in which our consumption habits are part and parcel of our processes of psycho-spiritual maturation, repentance, and the active cultivation of the virtues of prudence and temperance. If adopted on a wider scale the ascetic values and practices of Orthodox Christianity—amongst self-professing "Orthodox Christians," but also those who do not identify with the tradition—may significantly contribute to the amelioration of the global ecological crisis. When one thinks of Orthodox Christian asceticism amongst the laity living in the social sphere, one's mind will often turn toward the personal acts of fasting, charity, and prayer. Yet, although such engagements of self with the world and the divine hold immense spiritual benefit on a personal level for her who practices the faith, those who do not can still find ecological wisdom within both the principles and practices that guide Orthodox asceticism. The practice of fasting is something

---

139 Ecumenical Patriarch Bartholomew, Address at the Environmental Symposium, Santa Barbara, California, USA, November 8, 1997.
140 Herman Daly and Kenneth Townsend, eds., *Valuing the Earth: Economics, Ecology, Ethics* (Cambridge, MA: MIT Press, 1993).

which Orthodox Christianity shares with other faiths and which has largely been lost within the secular world (other than for personal physical or mental health), yet which is guided by principles that may help enable the entire global society to transition to a more ecologically sound mode of being. While personal fasting alone will not suffice when it comes to solving the ecological crisis, when engaged in communally and contemplatively, this ascetic practice has the ability to cultivate a more ecologically mindful civilizational ethos, produce ecologically beneficial consequences, and enable the recognition of principles of consumption that may be incorporated into our socio-economic models.

Ascetic Consumption

Within the collection of classic texts of Orthodox Christian spirituality, called the *Philokalia*, we find some of the most robust philosophies on consumption in discussions of fasting, in which cultivating *nepsis,* or a state of psycho-spiritual "watchfulness," "wakefulness," or "mindfulness," plays an integral role in the transformative dimensions of this ascetic exercise. *Nepsis* is described as vigilantly guarding one's heart and mind from vicious thoughts such as anger, jealousy, rage, despair, gluttony, greed, egoism, and lust. It is the practice of *nepsis* that helps enable one to transform these *pathê*, or pathological thoughts, into more reasonable desires and place them in the service of attaining the higher-order desire for the good. *Nepsis* is used in the sense of attentive watchfulness over our heartfelt desires, and in the case of fasting, the exercise literally entails "watching what we eat" as she who fasts attempts to control her appetitive desires. For those living within society, fasting places *nepsis* in the external social and physical world as the one fasting must make choices over what and how to consume. Fasting can enable one to become vigilantly attentive both to that which influences her own behaviors and how we influence our social and ecological environments, and can make us become more aware of the role that consumption plays in moral life.

In the current socio-economic status quo, production is designed to surpass the level of need and any naturally occurring desire for the goods produced or services rendered. This is where marketing and advertising function to intentionally tempt and or manipulate the population by appealing to their appetites, vanity, sense of low self-worth, and other vices as a means of manufacturing a sense of "need" for the newly overproduced goods and services so that they can continue the cycles of perpetual consumption-fueled growth. The logic behind such consumeristic practices is to appeal to people's passions, or *pathê* (the pathological aspects of human desire), so that their desires become so strong that they are transformed and perceived as "needs" so that they will consume the products at greater levels of intensity. *Nepsis* enables one to resist succumbing to such avaricious forces as they promote continual over-consumption, and avoid falling into habits that are inherently gluttonous by keeping us vigilantly aware of these forces as well as our own power to deter their influence upon our behavior. To this end, the widespread practice of *nepsis* may assist in reforming the vicious aspects of our civilizational ethos by cultivating the virtues of prudence, temperance, and self-control.

Given that our civilizational ethos operates on the principles of a socio-economic mindset that views persons as consumers and construes its visions of "goodness" within a paradigm of infinite consumption, the habits and dispositions developed during fasting can be brought forth into concentric circles from the personal to the civilizational, and may even have a bearing upon the ways in which we understand and engage in economic behavior as we collectively cultivate the virtues of prudence, temperance, and self-control and practice forms of consumptive asceticism. While there are many spiritual benefits to contemplatively abstaining from certain foods, the Orthodox method of fasting (in which practitioners observe strict abstinence from most animal products) is also capable of fostering an awareness of our dependence on, and relationality with, other forms of life and the larger ecosystems that we are a part of. Fasting can cultivate a state of awareness of the value of other forms of biotic existence and ought to make us reflect upon our food sources; asking questions such as: Where does my food come from? Is it a factory farm engaging in unsustainable practices or an ecologically-minded family farm? Do my larger patterns of consumption play a causative role in harming ecological life or do they contribute to regenerative and sustainable methods of cultivation? Once we begin to ask such questions and truly reflect upon the acts of relating with, depending on, and symbiotically coexisting with other sacred lifeforms, humans can come to view themselves as living within an intricate web of sacred life and recognize their responsibility for sustaining that life's vitality. In this way we may begin to practice perpetual *nepsis*, being ever mindful of where our food and products were sourced and how they were produced, and be constantly attentive to whether or not our general patterns of consumptive behavior are contributing toward our pursuit of goodness and flourishing—both as individual persons and as a mutually dependent global civilization.

Satiety: From Eating to Economics

Fasting was never intended to occur without deep contemplation of the divine order of the cosmos. To fast is to be a part of a historical community engaged in an ascetic practice and hence, ought to propel us to seek wisdom from those who have done so vigorously and with piety in the past. In what may seem an unexpected source of economic insight, the theological reflections on fasting found within the *Philokalia* may even be able to speak to the very principles governing our socio-economic models in that they both address consumption. For instance, Saint Gregory of Sinai discusses the ways in which those striving for virtue ought to partake of food; or in other words, how one pursuing the good life ought to consume.

Although he has individual persons in mind, Gregory's ideas can come to influence our understanding of collective consumption as well. Gregory delineates three degrees of consumption that remain below the level of sin:

1) *Self-Control*: in which one still desires to consume more, yet through self-discipline refrains from doing so. On a personal level we must all practice self-control and must not succumb to either our own desires for consumptive pleasure or the temptations of those seeking the maximization of profits who entice us to consume more of their products.

2) *Sufficiency*: by which one neither desires to consume more, yet is not rendered lethargic by his consumption, and hence is easily able to engage in other forms of activity after having consumed. This would be when a particular society or community has enough resources to achieve economic stability and has found a way to maintain ecological sustainability.

3) *Satiety*: in which one's consumption has made her feel lethargic, or slightly weighted down. Being satiated, one does not have enough physical or mental energy to perform other types of activity to the best of her abilities. Satiety on a collective level would entail using our resources to the point where we run at slight deficiencies from time to time yet,

when the collective does not continually verge on depletion, as we currently are.[141]

Gregory immediately goes onto to say that "to eat again after reaching satiety is to open the doors of gluttony."[142] With its focus on exponentially growing in a material manner that relies on perpetually consuming novel material goods and producing non-reusable waste, the neoclassical/neoliberal economic system is one which promotes a civilizational ethos and way of life whereby we are living well beyond the notion of satiety, and in which the virtues of temperance and moderation have almost become unfathomable given the demands of a system that fosters greed, insatiable desire, self-conceit, and disregard for life, and that functions on constant destruction, production, and disposal.

Our current neoclassical/neoliberal economic models actively deny the principle of satiety, and hence, are inherently at odds with Gregory of Sinai's understanding of virtuous consumption. The absence of a principle of satiety in regards to our civilization's consumption practices and economic models illustrates how our adherence to a neoclassical socio-economic paradigm fails to keep us on the path toward becoming good and growing closer in our relationship with the divine. The irony is that we often push the limits of what we consider to be the boundaries of sufficiency

---

141 Gregory of Sinai, *On Prayer*, in *The Philokalia*, vol. 4, eds. G. E. H. Palmer, Philip Sherrard, and Kallistos Ware (London: Faber & Faber, 1995), p. 281.
142 Gregory of Sinai, *On Prayer*, in *The Philokalia*, vol. 4, p. 281.

and satiety—as we pursue wealth and engage in consumption—because we do so as means of attaining what we perceive to be "the good life."[143] We naturally desire flourishing and well-being and strive to have lived well. Yet, what we often fail to realize is that non-regenerative growth and consumption practices that create non-revitalizing waste are antithetical to the ways in which we witness life's flourishing in the patterns of Nature. This leads us to misconceive the means of attaining our actual goals of existing in the re-creative and cooperative types of work and economic activities that are more imitative of those of the divine order and which will truly place us on a path toward the good. As the ecological economist Herman Daly writes:

> There is a limit to how many goods we can enjoy in a given time period, as well as a limit to our stomachs and the sensory capacity of our nervous systems. … By its "non-satiety" postulate, neoclassical economics formally denies the concept of the futility limit [when the utility of production falls to zero]. However, studies have shown that, beyond a "sufficiency threshold," both self-evaluated happiness and objective indices of welfare cease to increase with GDP.[144]

Neither our happiness nor our welfare—neither flourishing nor well-being—are being attained by our overly consumptive economic pursuits. If we are neither happier nor have increased our welfare, and we are also causing harm to other ecological life and

---

143 Northcott, *The Environment and Christian Ethics*, 73–79.
144 Daly, "Economics for a Full World," 6.

our own existence on earth, what is the purpose of such activities? We have now come to learn that in the long term we will further decrease our chances of attaining a life abundantly full of physical, psychological, and communal vitality if we continue to deny the importance of the virtues of temperance and moderation in our socio-cultural ethos, and as a result our socio-economic practices.

Writing at the dawn of the neoliberal turn of our neoclassical economic system, the Orthodox theologian Stanley Harakas lamented,

> With the coming of the affluent society and the emphasis on an ever larger Gross National Product, frugality and the temperate use of this world's goods was downplayed. In fact, when you think about it, it was almost turned into a vice. ... The "get more, spend more" mentality had made a shambles of the old ethical ideals of frugality and temperance in reference to the material things of this life. ... What used to be called frugality or temperate living is now "ecological awareness" and "conservation values."[145]

Harakas was correct to be critical of society's overemphasis on "getting more" to achieve success, and how this led to the loss of temperance as a result of the pursuit of perpetual economic growth in the early 1980s. The seemingly mundane act of evaluating economic success based solely on the growth of GDP (GNP in Harakas' time) is not only a manifestation of economic avarice and civilizational

---

145 Stanley Harakas, *Contemporary Moral Issues Facing the Orthodox Christian* (Minneapolis: Life & Light Pub., 1982), 164.

gluttony, but is an example of a civilizational misunderstanding in that such financial goals are actually uneconomic.

In economics, the term "utility" signifies a state in which a population's needs, wants, and demands are satisfied and adequately met by the system. Alternatively, the term disutility signifies running at a cost, or in other words, a costly sacrifice in short-term profitability in order to increase production and consumption levels as a means of achieving a benefit in the foreseeable future. Disutility costs include using more labor, the loss of leisure time, exposure to pollutants or other dangers, the depletion of resources, and other such factors, all of which produce negative effects upon human health and well-being or which decrease short-term profitability. The notion of marginal utility is the point at which a population's needs and demands for goods and services have not only been met but have gone slightly beyond the point of being satisfied: it is a level of slight excess beyond satisfaction. Marginal disutility is likewise the point at which only the most minimal sacrifices to profitability are made in order to achieve what is perceived to be the "greater good," or increased production or consumption. *The optimal state is when marginal utility and marginal disutility have reached an equilibrium so that the scales of consumption and production have met one another and achieved a balance.* Beyond this point of equilibrium, economic growth will only cause drastic increases in disutility and hence, the system itself will have failed to be properly managed and therefore becomes "*uneconomical.*" This is the point that we have currently reached.[146] Neoclassical economics, especially in its neoliberal form, has reached the point of being uneconomical, because it is not designed to achieve balance but is rather designed to pursue limitless and perpetual growth. This is a core problem with our current system: it is designed for infinite material growth in a finite biosphere. The prosperity of such a system is logically untenable in the long term.

Under current models of calculating GDP (Gross Domestic Product), if a new industry establishes itself in a particular region, thereby purchasing land, creating jobs, and possibly creating revenue for the local construction industry and real estate markets through housing development, we rightfully include these "positive" factors in the calculation of an increase in GDP. However, if that new industry begins to pollute local groundwater and air and thereby increases levels of illness, which in turn causes an increase in the "consumption" of medical services and pharmaceutical products in the region, these negative factors also contribute to an increase in GDP despite the fact that they in no way can be argued to be beneficial or contribute to human well-being, let alone flourishing. Ultimately, we must recognize that GDP is not an accurate indicator of human well-being and discover ways in which our economic calculations can go beyond the financial realm to incorporate genuine human well-being into how we determine what is best.

---

146 Herman Daly, *Ecological Economics and Sustainable Development: Selected Essays of Herman Daly* (Northampton, MA: Edward Elgar Pub., 2007).

As a means of remedying this situation, ecological economists have proposed the implementation of an indicator that would replace GDP, that would more accurately account for our genuine flourishing and well-being by including factors such as pollution, resource depletion, long-term environmental and social damage, poverty levels, and public health (especially the negative health effects caused by environmental pollution) into its calculations. What Herman Daly and John Cobb initially called the "Index of Sustainable Economic Welfare,"[147] and later referred to as a "Genuine Progress Indicator"[148] (GPI), would represent a more accurate depiction of the ways in which our economic activity is actually contributing to, or diminishing, a society's quality of life and well-being. A GPI would account for these negative factors as a counterbalance to financial growth and represent humanity's social and ecological well-being more accurately. While genuine flourishing cannot be measured empirically, the GPI would at least be capable of measuring the basic elements needed to create just social conditions and healthy environments that are more conducive to the common good. By including both human and ecological well-being in its purview, we can view a GPI as more than a simple alteration of our conceptual instruments of measurement. A GPI can serve as a pedagogical tool that can help us recognize just how codependent and interrelated we as humans are with the

---

147 Daly and Cobb, *For the Common Good*, 443.
148 Herman Daly, *From Uneconomic Growth to a Steady-State Economy* (Northhampton, MA: Edward Elgar Publishing, 2014), 64.

living ecological reality in which we find ourselves for our own well-being and begin to actually value nature. As an empirical tool, a GPI can help us become more mindful of our dependency on nature for our own well-being and may enable us to cultivate a more grateful disposition toward the natural world and all that it does for humankind.

A Eucharistic Disposition

Economically, we currently perpetuate a system in which we place no actual value on the externalities of a business's functional model, whereby natural resources are often viewed as essentially "free" inputs into the system. We then ungratefully utilize these resources as if they had no value until they are combined with human labor in the processes of production. It is the commodities and artifacts that were produced from natural resources that accrue value as interchangeable objects in the market, which then confer value upon natural environments as if their only worth is as storehouses of raw materials rather than as living systems that are beautiful in their own right as well as necessary for human flourishing and prosperity—not to mention existence and survival in the long run.

The Orthodox theologian John Zizioulas has claimed that the sacrality of created life bestows upon it a "uniqueness" that makes it "irreplaceable."[149] To be unique and irreplaceable is the antithesis

---

149 John Zizioulas, "Priests of Creation," 287.

of what it means for something to be a commodity, which is inherently fungible, or interchangeable. A commodity is a product, an objectified entity resulting from human labor, the value of which is determined by factors external to itself, such as demand for its use and efforts of labor exerted in its production or cultivation. The very idea of a commodity necessarily entails a utilitarian evaluation of its purpose in a system of trade where it is exchanged for other fungible objects; interchangeability and replaceability are integral features of commodification. If created life does indeed possesses sacrality, then to allow for the commodification of living beings and natural ecosystems in this manner is to neglect their sacrality as uniquely created lifeforms. Living beings and ecosystems cannot simultaneously be commodified in this way, and thereby objectified and solely valued instrumentally, and sincerely respected as intrinsically valuable—let alone sacred—beings.

As the ecological economist Herman Daly has been arguing for decades, the biosphere is finite and is the actual living system in which all other socially-constructed systems developed by humanity actually operate. The problem with neoclassical economics is that it has omitted biospheric finitude from its theoretical calculations and has an inherent tendency to treat natural resources as an infinite supply of potential raw inputs into the economy. Although natural ecosystems are indeed regenerative, they are only naturally capable of regeneration at a particular rate, beyond which our use of them hinders, or even terminates, their natural regenerative capacities. By viewing natural resources and the ecosystems in which they are found as either free inputs into the system of economic production or as inherently interchangeable entities, neoclassical economics simply seeks to replace one natural resource with another if and when the former is depleted, with no means of genuinely accounting for any of the negative effects that depletion or eradication might have caused to ecosystems or humankind.[150]

We must cultivate a disposition of *eucharistia*, or gratitude, that may come to influence the ways in which we economically value other forms of biotic and abiotic existence. If all of the natural world possesses an intrinsic value,[151] humans must be grateful for the innumerable and invaluable services, such as watersheds, carbon capture and oxygen production, sources of medicine, and food production, to name a few, that ecological systems provide for humanity's existence, survival, and flourishing. We must come to recognize that there exists a *natural diakonia* of the ecological services that the natural world provides for humanity and be grateful for it. In this sense, humanity needs to adopt a more *eucharistic disposition* toward nature, so that global civilization comes to view consumption as a life-affirming act that is appreciative of the living energies and living systems that make human life and flourishing

---

150 Herman Daly, "Economics for a Full World."
151 Intrinsic value, from the Orthodox Christian perspective, is viewed as a degree of sacrality due to the natural world being permeated by uncreated divine energies.

possible by seeking to replenish ecological vitality, rather than destructively devouring the natural world.

One way in which we can actively express our gratitude is by incorporating the notion of "natural capital"[152] into our economic models.

> *Natural capital* includes all the familiar resources used by humankind: water, mineral, oil, trees, fish, soil, air et cetera. But it also encompasses living systems, which include grasslands, savannas, wetlands, estuaries, oceans, coral reefs, riparian corridors, tundras, and rainforests.[153]

Incorporating the notion of natural capital into our economic models places an economic value upon the services that living organisms and natural resources provide for any processes of production or extraction. This means that the economic costs of harming ecosystems are factored into financial considerations and will reduce the degree to which we cause harm to nature by rendering many practices, such as fracking, mountaintop removal for coal, deforestation, the use of chemical fertilizers, and overfishing, as ultimately being economically unprosperous. Hence, using a GPI would more accurately reflect the ecological reality of our industrial practices. By valuing ecosystem services within our economic calculations, we can begin to develop practical ways of

---

152 Paul Hawken et al., *Natural Capitalism: Creating the Next Industrial Revolution* (New York: Hachette Book Group, 1999); Daly, *From Uneconomic Growth to a Steady-State Economy*, 45.
153 Hawken et al., *Natural Capitalism*, 2.

demonstrating our gratitude for natural *diakonia* within our daily socio-economic lives. Ultimately, in order to truly repent we must reform our current socio-economic system and begin implementing *ecological economic notions* such as *natural capital*, *satiety limits*, and a *GPI*, as we reorient the goal of our economic behavior from perpetual growth to one that is more stable and recognizes satiety as an ethical limit.

Conclusion

In September of 2017 Patriarch Bartholomew and Pope Francis of the Roman Catholic Church issued a joint letter[154] in which they denounced greed for limitless profit in markets as one of the primary sources of ecological devastation. In this article I have attempted to *emphasize* the fact that it is *not simply the vice of greed on the individual personal level* that is the primary problem but that *there is a systemic problem with the notion of unlimited growth that makes individual "greed," so to speak, inevitable in our current socio-economic system.* In sum, our ecological sin is a collective and systemic sin, which even morally decent persons partake in—be it in a voluntary or even involuntary fashion. As I have attempted to demonstrate, collective sin is not merely an aggregate of individual actions or even behaviors. *Collective Ecological Sin* is primarily the result of a pervasive attitude amongst persons whereby moral and social responsibility is persistently shifted away from either

---

154 Ecumenical Patriarch Bartholomew and Pope Francis, Joint Message on the World Day of Creation, September 1, 2017.

themselves on an individual level or, on small localized communal levels, toward more abstract and indeterminate entities, and in which people acquiesce to a system missing the mark of goodness and fail to adopt an ethos capable of reorienting our socio-economic trajectory and our personal sense of responsibility. Without both a set of intimate interpersonal relations and a sense of belonging to a larger ecological and intergenerational community, we overlook an integral aspect of who we are as moral agents in the world. When we develop a sense of moral identity as integral to who we are as persons and communities and who we identify as, living well becomes a matter of striving for personal and civilizational excellence in pursuit of the good life.

6. A LOOK AT INTERNATIONAL ENVIRONMENTAL LAW: TOWARDS WHAT GOALS?

Vincenzo Buonomo

Ecological Awareness in the Face of Environmental Degradation

How can international action on education be linked to the needs that routinely arise for the protection of the different ecosystems that coexist in our "common home"? And again, how does the environmental protection achieved through international norms and the action of the institutions of the international community relate to the directives present in *Laudato Si'*? In particular, then, how do they relate to the activities promoted to foster environmental awareness in the educational sector so as to provide an adequate response to the needs of people, communities, and states? These are the complex and pressing questions to which we will try to give some answers in these reflections. We have no presumption of being exhaustive; our aim is to provide critical and in-depth insights.[155]

It is first of all necessary to describe the background to the approach of international environmental law and practice.[156] Environmental protection engages the international legal system in terms of protection and prevention, conservation and preservation, as well as valorization and recovery, that at this point has configured a specific system of rules designed to adequately guarantee an interest now consolidated in the practice of relations between states and considered common to humanity. In this sense, the consideration made by the International Court of Justice may be enlightening: when called upon to pronounce on the use of atomic weapons, it rather dwelt on the effects of such means of warfare on the environment, describing it as "the space in which human beings live and on which their quality of life and health, including that of future generations, depends."[157] Therefore, every international activity is obliged to consider the close connection between human life on earth and the protection of the different ecosystems that make living conditions possible and contribute to the natural environment.

---

155 Contained and organized here are the reflections that formed the basis for the lectures given at the Advanced Training Course for the Joint Diploma in Integral Ecology, established by the Pontifical Roman Universities and Athenaeums.
156 The term "environmental" is paradigmatic to understand international action, which, built around the functional approach, has not yet fully embraced the expression "common home" on which the teaching of *Laudato Si'* is instead based.
157 *Legality of the Threat or Use of Nuclear Weapons: Advisory Opinion*, July 8, 1996 (in CIJ, *Recueil 1996*, 241–242).

Here we can immediately take up the essential passage of *Laudato Si'* on ecological action, expressed by an interesting interpretative methodology regarding issues of global relevance that affect the environment, such as climate change, agricultural work, the use of new technologies, the right to water, the loss of biodiversity, the overpopulation of the planet, and the sustainability of all development. The specific vision of the encyclical rests on the need to adopt radically new behaviors and lifestyles: "Many things have to change course, but it is we human beings above all who need to change" (LS, §202).

In this regard, the paradigm used by Pope Francis is that of integral ecology, with a reading and vision of the processes that affect nature with its balances and resources, a paradigm anchored in a firm anthropological foundation that allows both a reading of the facts and a vision of the future, and which requires "taking time to recover a serene harmony with creation, reflecting on our lifestyle and our ideals" (LS, §225). The person therefore remains the element that unites all analysis and therefore all actions aimed at rebalancing the relationship between the activity in the educational sector, the availability of resources to carry it out, and the protection of our common home. This could be useful, first of all, to make everyone more accountable, each in their different tasks and responsibilities. Furthermore, this orientation serves to base educational development and training on an anthropological dimension so as to overcome the barriers posed to international cooperation by limited resources, by different levels of technology, or by special interests and oppositions. Its adoption in the international framework of the 2030 Agenda for Sustainable Development is one more reason to move in this direction.

This approach explains why environmental care engages the international legal system in terms of protection, conservation, and enhancement, configuring it as a specific system of rules to adequately guarantee an interest that is now consolidated in the practice of relations between states and considered common to humanity.[158] In fact, in the process of development and elaboration of international rules in the contemporary era, environmental care has gradually taken its place as one of the essential fields for an ordered coexistence in the international community, that is, as a point of reference for the construction of an international order truly consonant with the full development of the person and peoples, as well as the affirmation of the role of civil society including in international relations.

The role of civil society has now been structured as an essential component not only in terms of monitoring and evaluating what is happening in terms of commitment, but also because a lack of attention to the decisions that are made weakens the impulse

---

158 More in-depth information in David B. Hunter, James Salzman, and Durwood Zaelke, eds., *International Environmental Law and Policy*, 3rd ed. (New York: Foundation Press, 2007); Alexandre Charles Kiss and Dinah Shelton, eds., *Guide to International Environmental Law* (The Hague: Nijhoff, 2007); Michel Prieur and Claude Lambrechts, eds., *Les hommes et l'environnement: Quels droits pour le XXIe siecle?* (Paris: Ed. Frison-Roche, 1998).

needed to make decisions in line with real needs. At the international level, the unequivocal tendency is to safeguard the "environmental heritage," as a synthesis between the ecological conscience actually matured in civil society and expressed by public opinion and the world of science, and the application of legal norms that, with a progressive erosion of state authority, are increasingly oriented towards protection of the various ecosystems. It is a tendency that has emerged because of the need to protect the environment from, or at least to minimize the risks arising from, economic, production, or resource exploitation choices, starting with energy sources, with the potential imbalances that are also manifested "in the conflicts generated by the lack of resources and in so many other problems that do not find sufficient space on the world's agendas" (LS, §48). Moreover, the role assumed by natural resources in a visibly strategic key and thus as possible reasons for conflicts, even of a military nature, directly capable of threatening security and peace, should not be overlooked.[159] It is enough here to refer to the danger of "the control of water by large global corporations becoming a major source of conflict" (LS, §31).

Another factor that contributed to defining international regulations was the changes in strategies and regulatory principles

---

159 This last aspect, although deprived of the geopolitical connotations of the superpower system, is still visible today in the form of economic-commercial relations between resource holders and users. Interesting on this topic are the data and considerations contained in Wolfgang Sachs and Tilman Santarius, eds., *Fair Future: Resource Conflicts, Security and Global Justice* (Black Point: Fernwood Publishing, 2007).

that occurred in relations between developed areas and the global South in which the ecological problem. Initially, in fact, cooperation with developing countries referred to the environment, but rather in the context of assistance and aid, perhaps linked to emergency situations in which only a humanitarian approach prevailed in the face of disasters or adverse environmental conditions: drought, desertification, erosion, flooding, and other alarming situations. Only more recent phenomena in their gravity, such as the discovery of the hole in the ozone layer, transboundary pollution, and climate change, have brought the link between environmental protection and cooperation activities into reality, placing rich and poor countries on the same level at least as far as the effects of environmental damage are concerned.

International Environmental Law between Principles and Courses of Action

International regulation is therefore subsidiary in nature, i.e., useful not only to the state apparatus, but to a broader relationship involving communities and individuals, even in their collective forms. Added to this is the fact that environmental problems cannot be confined to technical aspects alone, but arise as an expression of political, economic, and legal relations between the members of the international community. This substantial peculiarity of international environmental law, and the consequent systematic nature of its rules, can be founded on the maturation of a conviction in the early 1980s, according to which "humanity is part of nature and life depends on the uninterrupted functioning of natural systems that are sources of energy and food."[160] This approach reshapes the existing debate, particularly concerning the conduct of states, divided between the attitude of finding answers to environmental issues only within the framework of their own domestic legislation, and at the opposite end of the spectrum, the tendency to internationalize all types of protection. Around this duality, which is often conflicting, still revolves the whole process of ascertaining critical issues and thus developing guidelines and particular regulations within the framework of the international order.

This has been very clearly evidenced by the gradual maturation that international environmental law and practice—conservation, protection, recovery—have undergone since the conclusions of the United Nations Conference on the Human Environment (Copenhagen 1972), from which a twofold path can be discerned. The first approach is the tendency to envisage and prepare a *framework legislation* within which the will and consequent actions of states on the matter should converge. Framework legislation aims to define objective criteria formulated on the basis of principles that are generally recognized by all subjects of the international legal order or towards which at least an *opinio iuris* is deemed to exist. The second approach, on the other hand, remains oriented towards the definition of *sector-specific norms*, i.e., referring to individual

---

160 *World Charter for Nature*, Introduction (adopted with the Resolution 37/7 by the General Assembly on October 28, 1982).

aspects included in the broader scope of the environmental issue. In fact, the conduct rules are aimed at those particular areas where the states' interests are directly at stake, i.e., aspects that have limited scope for exclusive intervention by the domestic laws and policies of individual countries. The sector-specific approach, while responding to real needs, has the disadvantage of being too fragmented, and thus a source of standards—and consequent behavior—may differ between countries or groups of countries, rather than setting common standards as is the case with framework legislation.

Looking at the potential and effects of these regulations as a whole, it is clear that they now constitute an autonomous and self-sufficient field, while maintaining the necessary openness to other regulatory fields. Doctrinal positions speak of environmental legislation as *self-contained regimes* or identify it as *lex specialis* due to its ability to regulate every aspect of its applicability. In addition, still on the strictly rule-based side, with the elaboration of agreements, the takeover of customary norms, up to general principles, there is now a clear interpretative tendency to consider certain basic principles concerning the environment and its protection as generally accepted:

- the principle *of permanent sovereignty over natural resources*, which is part of the broader function of sovereignty exercised by the state over its territory and which is expressed through

the freedom to carry out—or allow to be carried out—certain activities, such as the use of land and water, and the exploitation of natural resources;
- the principle of *non-use of a state's territory to cause harm to others*, which constitutes a limitation of state action, restricting an absolute conception of sovereignty and not only because of the interest of other states, but also because of a more general obligation to protect the various ecosystems within it;
- the principle of *prevention* (or *preventive action*), which implies an obligation for states or those operating within them to act responsibly and bear the costs of avoiding any detrimental effect on environmental balances;
- the *precautionary* principle (also in the form of the *precautionary approach*), which takes the form of a series of obligations in the face of serious, even irreversible, risks to the environment or, in the absence of certain scientific and technical data that may require prior authorization, prior assessment of the impact of behavior and actions or transparency in information;
- the principle of *common but differentiated responsibility*, which understands the common responsibility towards the environment that states are called upon to implement in light of their different levels of development and socio-economic situation;

- the principle of *compensation for environmental damage* (*polluter pays*), according to which whoever compromises the environment by their activity is obliged to restore the situation prior to the damage done and to pay compensation for it;
- the principle of *cooperation* as a broader obligation, which is closely linked to the concept of sustainable development that requires balancing the needs of development with environmental protection.[161]

These principles form the basis of the institutions of international environmental law. The tendency—while remaining *de jure condendo*—is indeed to consider them as determining obligations in absolute terms (*erga omnes*),[162] some of which tend to be configured as non-derogable, if not by norms of equal rank, thus placing them in the category of international *jus cogens*.[163] Leaving aside the doctrinal debates, this means that the

---

161 For an in-depth discussion of the aforementioned principles, please refer to Nicolas de Sadeleer, *Environmental Principles:From Political Slogans to Legal Rules* (Oxford: Oxford University Press, 2002); Sumudu A. Atapattu, *Emerging Principles of International Environmental Law* (Ardsley, NY: Transnational Pub., 2006), especially 203ff.

162 On this category of *erga omnes obligations* applied to environmental issues, see Christian J. Tams, *Enforcing Obligation Erga Omnes in International Law* (Cambridge: Cambridge University Press, 2005), 120; Philippe Sands, *Principles of International Environmental Law*, 2nd ed. (Cambridge: Cambridge University Press, 2003), 188ff.

163 On the necessary care not to consider as mandatory (*jus cogens*) any kind of obligation that may arise in international relations, see the critical position of James Crawford, *Multilateral Rights and Obligations in International Law*, Recueil des Cours 319 (Leiden: Nijhoff, 2006), 408ff.

environmental issue has changed some traditional assumptions of the international order, starting with the notion that in the face of a norm, the behavior of a subject of that order responds to the principle of reciprocity and the existence of bilateral or reciprocal obligations assumed by other subjects. In environmental matters, in fact, the category of *collective interest* can be seen to be operative, which is expressed in the motivations and effects of international legislation, whether agreed or customary, an interest that clearly goes beyond the conduct and attitude of the individual country. Such an interest is embodied in the idea that the environment— and its various ecosystems—should be considered as a *common heritage*, towards which domestic jurisdiction must necessarily correlate with global conduct.

The concept of common heritage matured in the international legal order because of the protection of collective goods or goods that are considered to belong to humanity itself.[164] This is an orientation that in the light of international practice is neither a mere guideline, nor a utopia in the face of individual state sovereignties that perceive their power over their respective territories with a patrimonial projection:[165]

---

164 On the origin and further development of this concept see Kemal Baslar, *The Concept of the Common Heritage of Mankind in International Law* (The Hague: Nijhoff, 1999); Alexandre Kiss, *La notion de patrimoine commun de l'humanité*, Recueil des Cours 175 (Leiden: Nijhoff, 1982), 99–256. For the area of international codification of the law of the sea, see United Nations, *The Law of the Sea: Concept of the Common Heritage of Mankind* (New York, 1987).
165 See Philippe Kahn, "Les patrimoines communes de l'humanité: quelques réflexions," in *Les hommes et l'environnement: Quels droits pour le XXIe siecle?*, ed.

Every ecological approach needs to incorporate a social perspective which takes into account the fundamental rights of the poor and the underprivileged. The principle of the subordination of private property to the universal destination of goods, and thus the right of everyone to their use, is a golden rule of social conduct. (LS, §93)

This orientation may represent a way to view, from a legal-political point of view, the existence of assets—environmental assets—that need protection or at least a guarantee of common protection, since even if they are present or located on territories subject to state sovereignty, they constitute an asset for all: natural resources, marine, and biological diversity are some of the possible examples.[166] This is why contemporary international law—in spite of objective difficulties—has fostered a change in the behavior of states from the attitude of "not doing something" to the obligation to "do something" in relation to the environment, but with the objective of protecting it, unlike previously.[167] Everything, therefore,

---

Michel Prieur and Claude Lambrechts (Paris: Ed. Frison-Roche, 1998), 306–314.
166 See in this respect also P. S. Rao, "Environment as a Common Heritage of Mankind: a Policy Perspective," in United Nations, *International Law on the Eve of the Twenty-First Century: Views from the International Law Commission* (New York, 1997), 201–216.
167 An example of this was the expression contained in the General Agreement on Tariffs and Trade (GATT) of 1947, which stated the States Parties' objective of the "complete utilization of the world's resources" (Preamble), modified by the Marrakesh Accords (1995) establishing the World Trade Organization (WTO), successor to the GATT, which spoke of the "optimal utilization of the world's resources" and the compatibility of this utilization with sustainable development. For an extensive discussion of the relationship between WTO activity and the

because of a superior interest that is configured as a collective interest in relation to a part, the environment, of the *common heritage of humanity*.[168]

Educating the Consciences of People and Peoples

If, as mentioned above, certain principles are now generally accepted (permanent sovereignty over natural resources; non-use of the territory of one state to cause harm to others; prevention; precaution; common but differentiated responsibility; cooperation) with regard to the rules of existing multilateral conventions, it is possible to divide them into three categories with regard to the legal effects produced with respect to the states that adhere to them: rules that create an *obligation of conduct*;[169] rules that create

---

environment, see the various essays in Sandrine Maljean-Dubois, ed., *Droit de l'Organisation Mondiale du Commerce et protection de l'environnement* (Brussels: Bruylant, 2003).

168 This argument could be read as an abstract or meta-legal category, while it can be proposed as an example of an explanation of the progressive self-consciousness of the international community—and therefore of the various peoples that make it up—that emerges in relation to areas and situations within it and consequently as to the corresponding principles that regulate them. On the concept of the common heritage of mankind, there is then a broad doctrinal and normative elaboration, now consolidated, even in the presence of sometimes differing interests and practices in international relations. See on this topic Willem Riphagen, "The International Concern for the Environment as Expressed in the Concepts of the 'Common Heritage of Mankind' and of 'Shared Natural Resources,'" in *Trends in Environmental Policy and Law*, ed. Michel Bland (Gland: IUCN, 1980), 343ff. Cf. Kiss, *Droit international de l'environnement*, 19ff, on the relationship between environmental protection and the concept of the common heritage of mankind.

169 For example, the 1960 Convention for the Protection of Workers against

a *ban*;[170] *policy* rules.[171] Of course, it should not be forgotten that very often, despite formal agreement, the states' actions do not seem to fully embrace these provisions, preferring behavior that is not only detrimental to the norms themselves but especially to the environmental situation: this cannot help but lead to considering the slow but progressive progress of the international legal system towards full respect for the ecosystem and its protection as ineffective.

Ionizing Radiation, the 1960 Convention on Third Party Liability in the Field of Nuclear Energy, the 1963 Convention on Civil Liability for Nuclear Damage, the 1969 Convention on Civil Liability for Oil Pollution Damage, the 1969 Convention on Intervention on the High Seas in Cases of Oil Pollution, the 1973 Convention on the Prevention of Pollution from Ships, the 1981 Convention on Occupational Safety and Health and the Working Environment, the 1979 Convention on the Physical Protection of Nuclear Material, the 1986 Convention on Early Warning of a Nuclear Accident.

170 For example, the 1963 Treaty on the Prohibition of Nuclear Tests in the Atmosphere, Outer Space and Underwater, the 1968 European Agreement on the Restriction of the Use of Certain Detergents in Washing and Cleaning of Certain Products, the 1971 Treaty on the Prohibition of the Use of Nuclear Weapons and Other Weapons of Mass Destruction on the Seabed and in their Subsoil, the 1971 Convention on the Prohibition of the Use of Ocean Floor and Subsoil, the 1976 Convention on the Prohibition of the Use of Environmentally Modifying Techniques for Military or Other Hostile Purposes, the 1989 Convention on the Prohibition of Bottom Trawling in the South Pacific.

171 For example, the 1974 Agreement for an International Energy Program, the 1980 European Convention on Transboundary Co-operation between Territorial Communities or Authorities, the 1980 Convention on Future Multilateral Co-operation in the North-East Atlantic Fisheries, the 1985 Protocol on Co-operation in Combating Marine Pollution in Emergencies in East Africa, the 1985 Agreement between the ASEAN Countries on the Conservation of Nature and Natural Resources, the 1992 Convention for the Protection of the Marine Environment of the North-East Atlantic, or the set of legal acts that concluded the 1992 Conference on the Protection of the Black Sea against Pollution.

But this requires an educational and conscience-building effort that starts with individuals and reaches the state and the entire international community: "Because the stakes are so high, we need institutions empowered to impose penalties for damage inflicted on the environment. But we also need the personal qualities of self-control and willingness to learn from one another" (LS, §214). In fact, even for environmental protection, the main problem of the international legal system lies in the relationship between state sovereignty and the natural environment: international environmental protection presupposes, in fact, an awareness that the choices of states and peoples are increasingly influenced by the factor of *interdependence*, which requires, as a response, measures of solidarity to be reflected on the legal level with rules that are either equivalent or at least of similar scope. Even a minimal assessment shows that this expectation seems to elude the conduct pursued by states on the level of commitments—even binding ones—adopted in the international legal order, since the path towards this awareness requires a prior step: the consideration of the concept of sovereignty not as a synonym for exclusive domination, the absolute power of the state within its borders, because this would be in direct opposition to an international protection of the environment. But how can we forget that at the moment, only the gravity of the problem has actually led to a limited concept of sovereignty? In the face of ecological damage, borders no longer provide protection,[172] whereas the prevention of damage implies that the state must also act actively for the benefit of the environmental protection of other states.

The context that reflects the current state of international law and in which intergovernmental institutions also move indicates certain priorities: the effects of the relationship between environmental degradation and poverty; the consequences on the environment caused by the lack of economic growth in vast areas of the planet; demographic pressure linked to the availability of resources; changed needs and consumer habits in developed areas; the working environment and health of populations living in rural or marginalized areas; the obstacles to environmental protection caused by the foreign debt of most developing countries.

Following the UN's adoption of the 2030 Agenda for Sustainable Development, it is clear that the main issue, which has been clear since the Rio Conference on Environment and Development in 1992, is certainly still economic and financial. This means: having the necessary political and legislative instruments within the individual states so that economic activity can be transformed into ecological production; a financial commitment of the more developed countries towards the poor countries; coordination of the demands of civil society organizations; a *sustainable development*

---

172 In this regard are interesting the considerations of Atul Kohli, Georg Sørensen, and Jeannie Sowers, "States and Sovereignty: Introduction," in Pamela S. Chasek, ed., *The Global Environment in the Twenty-First Century* (Tokyo: United Nations University Press, 2000), 15–21.

prerequisite; *governance* of the environmental issue; the need for specific regulations towards climate change, the protection of forests, and the protection of living species.

In spite of the limits posed by one-sided approaches, the international legal system has come to recognize the existence of international *standards* upon which to base the political and legislative behavior of individual states in environmental matters: the *precautionary approach* (or principle); *individual liability* for environmental damage (*polluter pays*); the *safety–environment* connection; and the necessary *progressive development* of international environmental law. To be effectively understood, these results must be included in the broader path that international environmental law has followed in its ongoing development, characterized by the transition from an exclusive focus on individual sectors to the definition of norms that address the dimension of the environmental problem in global terms; by regionalization in the conclusion of international agreements; and by the establishment of intergovernmental institutions for the general implementation of uniform standards, to the benefit of the aim of protecting different ecosystems. In this regard, *virtuous practices* can be considered as *examples* for identifying and assessing the effectiveness of international norms and their repercussions in domestic legal systems, such as liability for *environmental damage* with the corresponding obligations imposed on states; prior assessment of the consequences of an activity that may affect the environment;

contacts with nearby and neighboring states; the obligation to avoid a *double standard* in the legal regulation of damage caused by a country, or the possibility of access to information and administrative and judicial procedures in the country where the damage originated. On this last aspect relating to information, mention should be made of the Aarhus Convention on Access to Information, Public Participation in Decision-Making, and Access to Justice in Environmental Matters of 1998, the first multilateral regulatory act to impose obligations on states with regard to their residents' ability to be informed, participatory responsibility in decision-making processes, and the effects of legal action taken in relation to related or suffered damage.

Likewise, considering the guidelines of intergovernmental institutions, a significant example is the relationship between the environment and human rights which, despite the absence of a specific regulatory provision, has seen attempts at formalization both at the United Nations and in regional human rights protection systems. In particular, it is the new challenges placed in the path of the human family that demand *governance* capable of regulating and managing the new goals that individual countries reach on a daily basis, even in the specific area of environmental protection, adding to the obvious successes the demand for *rights* from subjects who are holders of such rights. And the right to the environment falls within this framework and can no longer be considered only among the possible *interests* of the individual; indeed it is now linked not only to the environmental issue in general, but also to its specifics.

Specialized Contribution and Global Dimension

The *ecological awareness* present in international relations and the degree of *progression* achieved so far by the international legal system[173] have, therefore, paved the way for a move towards legally binding forms of environmental protection, prioritizing that relational profile that, while essential to relations between states, is also a requirement expressed by the dignity of the individual.

The progress achieved by science and technology over the years, together with increasingly complex economic processes involving a growing number of countries, have been able to guarantee an ever-increasing level of development in the educational sector. But the existence of widespread poverty and the anxieties emanating from the most disadvantaged areas demand ever broader and more effective responses, accompanying the programs drawn up at the international level in an attempt to support all human activity—starting with those concerning the use of resources and hence the safeguarding of the goods of creation—and guide it towards the goal of "caring for the common home." And here lie the competences of intergovernmental institutions that operate in direct contact with the reality of the educational world in its various dimensions, taking care to act in a sustainable, ecologically

---

173 See the *Charter Of The United Nations*, art. 13.1.a).

compatible manner. A tangible fact, or rather a summary, is offered by Agenda 2030, which in Goal 4, in proposing the goal of quality, equitable, and inclusive education, to be achieved by guaranteeing learning opportunities for all, indicates among the other actions to be taken that of ensuring:

> That all learners acquire the knowledge and skills needed to promote sustainable development, including, among others, through education for sustainable development and sustainable lifestyles, human rights, gender equality, promotion of a culture of peace and non-violence, global citizenship and appreciation of cultural diversity and of culture's contribution to sustainable development. (Goal 4, 4.7)

In this regard, *Laudato Si'* offers a method, that of dialogue, which takes on a strategic and not merely conventional role because it becomes the carrier of the common good. Pope Francis says in this regard: "Today, in view of the common good, there is urgent need for politics and economics to enter into a frank dialogue in the service of life, especially human life" (LS, §189). Serving the individual—through literacy, study, and research—presents itself not only as a goal to be achieved, but as a constant indicator for activities that really aim to promote the common good:

> In the present condition of global society, where injustices abound and growing numbers of people are deprived of basic human rights and considered expendable, the principle of the common good immediately becomes, logically and inevitably,

a summons to solidarity and a preferential option for the poorest of our brothers and sisters. (LS, §158)

This call is the basis not only for the necessary relationships between people, but also the need for internationally coordinated actions to address issues such as environmental protection. In fact, the encyclical states that "the analysis of environmental problems cannot be separated from the analysis of human, family, work-related and urban contexts, nor from how individuals relate to themselves, which leads in turn to how they relate to others and to the environment" (LS, §141).

It is only by fully understanding this logic that it is possible to recognize one of the limits placed on action taken at the international level in the face of contemporary facts and situations that require environmental security. Too often, in fact, in addition to the absence of a formed conscience when faced with actual problems, it is forgotten that global development is one of the prerequisites for the individual well-being of peoples and individuals. The idea, already stated by Pope Francis in *Evangelii Gaudium*, returns. According to it, "the whole is greater than the part" (EG, §237) which stands alongside the principle that "unity is greater than conflict" (EG, §228). Its inclusion in international relations could facilitate a policy management and norm enforcement that is responsive to needs. This is where the need arises for full acceptance of the concept of sustainability in its definition of *sustainable development*. This concept began to emerge in international terminology in 1987 with the Bruntdland Report, which defined it as "development that meets the needs of the present without compromising the ability of future generations to meet their own needs."[174] Since then, it has appeared in acts and documents of the various institutions of the United Nations, and was then incorporated into specific policy and normative guidelines by the 1992 Conference on Development and the Environment, in particular the Rio Declaration[175] and further instruments, up to the 2030 Agenda.[176]

Then there is the capacity for dialogue and the related proposals called upon to involve the various sectors of international action, but we must bear in mind that in preparing studies and analyses, it is not possible to separate concepts from concrete situations. The risk is that interpretations will be limited, just as the actions taken will be limited because they will not be able to involve all the various protagonists in their diverse roles and responsibilities: "In the face of possible risks to the environment which may affect the common good now and in the future, decisions must be made based on a comparison of the risks and benefits foreseen for the various possible alternatives" (LS, §184). By educating for the protection of the common home, then, we refer to the special relationship between

---

174 World Commission on Environment and Development, *Our Common Future*, Italian translation (Milan: Bompiani, 1988), 71.
175 Sustainable development is mentioned in articles 1, 4, 5, 7, 8, 9, 12, 20, 21, 22, 24.
176 For an analysis of the concept of sustainable development and its effective scope in the context of international environmental law, see Nico Schrijver, *The Evolution of Sustainable Development in International Law: Inception, Meaning and Status* (Leiden: Nijhoff, 2008).

a society—made up of people, institutions, rules—and the nature in which it is embedded. Nature therefore cannot be considered "as something separate from ourselves or as a mere setting in which we live. We are part of nature, included in it and thus in constant interaction with it" (LS, §139). Even sector-specific training, aimed at defending different ecosystems or safeguarding biodiversity so as to conserve different species, will never be truly effective if we do not consider the social dynamics and thus the political, economic, cultural, social and, not least, spiritual indicators that characterize the reality of human societies. Nor will a climate agreement be adequate that does not include a conversion of people's behavior, industrial activity, and agricultural production, the latter including livestock and forests. The lack of a serious education and training process in fact leads to disengagement, which is the most obvious challenge that must be faced in the effort to protect the common home. Commitments made at the international level, in fact, risk remaining unfulfilled and not only because one country declares its withdrawal, but because there is a lack of concrete attention on the part of other states, starting with the necessary funding. This is the case with the Climate Agreement: in Paris, in 2015, the states made a commitment to resolve the issue of the use of coal as a source of energy with funding that was to reach $100 billion per year from 2018 onwards, so as to enable the gradual achievement of "carbon free." But today's figures show that this has not happened. Some states have justified their disengagement by attributing it to domestic economic situations, others to international contingencies. The fact is that to date, despite multiple and repeated declarations of intent, each country is waiting for another to take the first step, and no one is taking a direct initiative.

Dialogue: Towards a Coherent Human-Environment Relationship

By placing the primacy of education at the center of all action, the objection that environmental protection is subordinate to economic action or to a more general progress of societies is no longer valid. Moreover, international cooperation has now moved beyond the approach used in the 1960s and 1970s, when development was considered as an effect of economic growth, as indicated in the Declaration on Social Progress and Development adopted by the UN in 1969.[177] In this regard, the encyclical states:

> We need to grow in the conviction that a decrease in the pace of production and consumption can at times give rise to another form of progress and development. Efforts to promote a sustainable use of natural resources are not a waste of money, but rather an investment capable of providing other economic benefits in the medium term. If we look at the larger picture, we can see that more diversified and innovative forms

---

177 *Declaration* adopted with the Resolution AG 2542 (XXIV), on December 11, 1969, art. 7 says: "The rapid expansion of national income and wealth and their equitable distribution among all members of society are fundamental to all social progress."

of production which impact less on the environment can prove very profitable. It is a matter of openness to different possibilities which do not involve stifling human creativity and its ideals of progress, but rather directing that energy along new channels. (LS, §191)

This means that the environmental issue related to development policies in the educational sector must also be considered, necessarily, as global and only globally can it be addressed. This is underlined precisely by the close relationship—Pope Francis speaks of connection: "Everything in the world is connected" (LS, §16 and §117)[178]—between climate change, the decrease in the rate of schooling, and the dwindling resources for education and training, with the consequent increase in underdevelopment and poverty, including educational poverty. In other words, a cause-effect relationship is increasingly evident, according to which any action—preventive or consequent—to safeguard the environment cannot but encompass every possible human, economic, political, and scientific component that is able to contribute to combating educational insecurity and poverty in education. *Laudato Si'* warns in this regard: "Strategies for a solution demand an integrated approach to combating poverty, restoring dignity to the excluded, and at the same time protecting nature" (LS, §139).

---

178 It then specifically indicates the connection between environmental degradation and culture (cf. LS, §6), between creatures (cf. LS, §42), and between human and environmental degradation (cf. LS, §56).

Therefore, an approach to the increase of sustainable educational processes that wants to be functional and not instrumental, cannot be dictated by partial solutions or inspired by specific interests—of geographic area, economic sector, or business sector—but "It is essential to seek comprehensive solutions which consider the interactions within natural systems themselves and with social systems" (LS, §139). Underlying these solutions is the contribution of the policies of individual countries, as well as the directives and action plans of international institutions, their operational role, so as to formulate suitable solutions: "Global regulatory norms are needed to impose obligations and prevent unacceptable actions" (LS, §173). That's why, while dwelling on the evils and risks caused by environmental degradation, and reading about the damage caused to the education sector with its repercussions on literacy, schooling, and training, the encyclical does not limit itself to calling for changes in behavior and lifestyles, but presents *dialogue* as the method to follow, directing it towards five areas:

- development of cooperative action, which, despite a broad framework of analysis of the many problems, is summed up in the goal of eliminating the "gap" caused by poverty: "A more responsible overall approach is needed to deal with both problems: the reduction of pollution and the development of poorer countries and regions" (LS, §175);
- the promotion of new policies at the national level, overcoming the obstacles caused by corruption,

incompetence, the thirst for power, or the pursuit of sectoral interests that are often inhuman and disrespectful towards the protection of the common home: "A healthy politics is sorely needed, capable of reforming and coordinating institutions, promoting best practices and overcoming undue pressure and bureaucratic inertia" (LS, §181);

- decision-making processes in every aspect that can concern social living and therefore within it the environmental dimension (primary education, schooling, training), and the consequent threats due to the lack of transparency, sincerity, truth, and information in the name of immediate advantages that are solely economic. Through real dialogue between the different stakeholders, Pope Francis anticipates that "economic returns can thus be forecast more realistically, taking into account potential scenarios and the eventual need for further investment to correct possible undesired effects" (LS, §183);

- co-responsibility between politics and economics, which "tend to blame each other when it comes to poverty and environmental degradation," forgetting that, in the face of environmental catastrophe, it is necessary for both "to acknowledge their own mistakes and find forms of interaction directed to the common good" (LS, §198);

- understanding between religions and the empirical and natural sciences, aimed above all at a clear understanding of the role of scientific procedures and their explanation of reality, including the degradation of the common home. This means on the one hand an indispensable "dialogue among the various sciences is likewise needed, since each can tend to become enclosed in its own language, while specialization leads to a certain isolation and the absolutization of its own field of knowledge"; on the other hand, dialogue among believers, which should spur "religions to dialogue among themselves for the sake of protecting nature, defending the poor, and building networks of respect and fraternity" (LS, §201).

Dialogue "with all and among all": this is the call of the encyclical, a dialogue to which is entrusted the task of seeking common ways and paths to free the human family from the persistent anguish arising from the degradation of the common home due to a lack of sustainability education. And this starts from the responsibility of each person, from his or her daily commitment to do something to protect and preserve the common home. Through dialogue, therefore, it is possible to combat environmental degradation, going further in confronting those iniquitous behaviors that characterize our daily lives in different ways. It is no coincidence that the 2030 Agenda sets as its concluding goal, Goal 17, partnership, that is inclusive partnerships, built on principles and values, a common vision and shared goals, which put people and the planet at the centre, are needed at global, regional, national and local levels, something that only a serious and articulate dialogue can enable.

Certainly, criteria for action will be needed to address the different needs of the common home in a global way, looking at sustainability as an effect of solidarity between generations, so that environmental protection also becomes care for the whole of humanity of today and tomorrow. Pope Francis recalls in this regard that an "an integral ecology is also made up of simple daily gestures which break with the logic of violence, exploitation and selfishness" (LS, §230).

7. THE RELATIONSHIP BETWEEN THE HOLY SEE AND THE ECUMENICAL PATRIARCHATE: A JOURNEY TOGETHER

Sandra Ferreira Ribeiro

First of all, thanks to God, and then to the organizers of this Summit for the important occasion it represents, not only for us Christians on the path of unity between our Churches, especially the Orthodox and Catholic Churches, but also for all humanity, which, more than ever, needs our witness of fraternity and a common commitment to the various challenges that threaten the future of the human family. I feel honored to be invited to participate and to be able to make a personal contribution.

The topic of the relationship between the Holy See of Rome and the Ecumenical Patriarchate of Constantinople would require several volumes, and indeed much literature has already been produced. Yet, there would always be many new things to say because the story of this relationship is part of God's story with mankind, of the story of the Church, which is both divine and human, and therefore always open to new understandings and insights.

Today we are gathered in a place of great value and significance for our Christian history, in a time that is chronological, historical, but which looks forward to a *kairòs* for the unity of the Churches and for the good of humanity that all of us Christians, united, are called to live and work for.

I would take Pope Francis' expression "Ecumenism is on the journey"[179] as the leitmotif of this short talk, relating it particularly to the common commitment that the Catholic and Orthodox Churches today, in the persons of Pope Francis and Patriarch Bartholomew, have taken on with reference to the safeguarding of creation, but describing the methodology of ecumenical dialogue in itself.

Remembering some of the decisive stages of this journey, I would like to mention the meeting between Pope Paul VI and Patriarch Athenagoras, of blessed memory, when on January 5, 1964, their meeting in Jerusalem was a symbolic event that consolidated the Copernican revolution inaugurated by modern ecumenism: relationships whose purpose is no longer the return of one Church to the other but of all to Christ. Both, starting from a different point, indeed, from "the West and the East ... called to meet in his name," as Athenagoras[180] expresses it, that is, starting

---

179   Pope Francis in *Papa Francesco* states: "Ecumenism is on the journey." The Holy See, October 12, 2016. Available at cistampa.com/story/papa-francesco-ribadisce-lecumenismo-si-fa-in-cammino-4416.

180   Patriarch Athenagoras and Pope Paul VI, *Tomos Agapis*, n. 48, p. 109.

from their own Church, their own Tradition, their own history, they head towards the same destination, Jerusalem, where Christ died and rose again, accomplishing the salvation of the world. Paul VI also has similar words when he says that "the two paths converge and arrive at the source of the Gospel."[181]

The Second Vatican Council on the Catholic side and the Rhodes Conferences on the Orthodox side, convened by Patriarch Athenagoras with the consent of the other primates, opened up the two Churches to the desire to get closer and begin a dialogue "on an equal footing," i.e., recognizing each other's ecclesiality. And the Fourth Conference, which took place in Chambésy in 1968, declared at its conclusion that the contacts and manifestations of charity between the two Churches would continue "so that the existing difficulties regarding a fruitful theological or theoretical dialogue might be definitively overcome."[182]

The journey of unity between the two Churches then began with what went down in history as the "Dialogue of Charity," which was not only the basis for a future theological dialogue between the two Churches, but its essence. In fact, the visible unity to be achieved between the Churches begins, continues, and reaches its apex precisely in the implementation of the Word of God, in returning over and over to Jerusalem, the place of Calvary, where the Cross

---

[181] Patriarch Athenagoras and Pope Paul VI, *Tomos Agapis*, n. 49.
[182] Patriarch Athenagoras and Pope Paul VI, *Tomos Agapis*, p. 487. Cf. also Pope John XXIII, Pope Paul VI, Patriarch Athénagoras I, Patriarch Dimitrios I, Pope John Paul II, *Le livre de la charité, 1958-1978* (Éditions du Cerf, 1984), p. 22.

was planted that made possible the unity of mankind with God and with each other; the place where the Church was born, the place of the Eucharist and the Trinitarian agape shared with us as a gift by the Holy Spirit; the place where the Word of God was fulfilled once and for all.

With regard to the theme of this Summit, both Patriarch Athenagoras and Paul VI died before seeing the dream of the celebration in the one chalice realized, but the pontiffs and patriarchs who succeeded them continued the "Dialogue of Charity." The theological dialogue officially began in 1980, under the pontificate of John Paul II and with the Ecumenical Patriarch Demetrios I.

For Athenagoras, unity among Christians was a priority in his life and writings. Already in January 1969, he spoke about the responsibility of Christians in the world, recalling an "us" of the united Church: "This is the hour of the Church: united, it must offer guidelines of hope to the world."[183]

The Ecumenical Patriarchate, always sensitive to the problems of humanity, has realized the seriousness of the ecological crisis as a threat to God's creation and to human beings themselves. Thus, in 1989, Patriarch Demetrios I, in an encyclical letter addressed to all Orthodox believers, all Christians, and all people of goodwill, "called for awareness of the seriousness of the ecological crisis and

---

183 Stefania Falasca, "Bartolomeo I e Francesco: Laudato si', un segno ecumenico," Avvenire.it, June 18, 2015, https://www.avvenire.it/opinioni/pagine/segno-ecumenico.

to act responsibly for the protection of God's material creation."[184] It also invited all Christian churches to observe September 1 as "a day of prayer and supplication to the Creator ... both as thanksgiving for the great gift of creation and as supplication for its protection and salvation."[185]

The topic is gaining more and more importance on the agenda of the churches. That same year, the Conference of European Churches and the Council of European Bishops' Conferences in the First European Ecumenical Assembly included the safeguarding of creation as a topic of common commitment.

In Seoul in 1990, an Ecumenical World Assembly "Towards Covenant Solidarity for Justice, Peace, and the Safeguarding of Creation"[186] took place. It brought together representatives of many churches, movements, and Christian communities from the various continents.

Also in 1990, John Paul II dedicated his Message for the World Day of Peace to the theme "Peace with God the Creator, peace with all creation," which was followed twenty years later by Benedict XVI with his Message "If you want to cultivate peace, protect creation."

---

184 Antonio Spadaro, "Liturgia cosmica ed ecologia: Intervista al Metropolita ortodosso Ioannis Zizioulas," *Civiltà cattolica* 3962 (2015): 164–176, at 168.
185 Cf. Luca Maria Negro, "Le Religioni e la terra – per un impegno attivo," February 17, 2022.
186 Cf. Assemblea Ecumenica Mondiale, "Verso la solidarietà dell'alleanza per la giustizia, la pace e la salvaguardia del creato," in Stefano Rosso and Emilia Turco, eds., *Enchiridion Oecumenicum: Consiglio Ecumenico delle Chiese, 5, Assemblee Generali 1948-1998* (Bologna: EDB, 2001), nn. 2387–2455, pp. 1541–1575.

Pope Benedict XVI took a great interest in and made the Catholic Church interested in ecology,[187] which earned him the nickname "Green Pope."

And in 2001 we have the *Charta Oecumenica* of Strasbourg which, echoing the invitation of Patriarch Demetrios, recommends "the establishment by the European Churches of an ecumenical day of prayer for the protection of creation."[188]

Thus the churches' awareness of their duty to reflect and make people aware of the ecological urgency is growing and deepening. But there is also growing awareness of uniting as one voice in doing so: not only in denouncing the institutional irresponsibility of the crisis, but in concern for humanity and its survival. Ecumenism, in fact, besides wanting to overcome the scandal of divisions, also stems from an awareness of the urgency of bringing the message of Christ, which is a message of peace, justice, kindness, and integral salvation for every person. And, in keeping with our faith in the Triune God, it is a message that calls for communion, fraternity, praise, and thanksgiving to God for life, for the whole of creation, which is a web of relationships woven with mutual love.

Many have already pointed out the similarity of origin of the terms "ecumenism" and "ecology": both have in their root the

---

187 Cf. one of his talks: Benedict XVI, "Safeguarding of Creation," General Audience, Palazzo Apostolico in Castel Gandolfo, Wednesday, August 26, 2009. Available at https://www.vatican.va/content/benedict-xvi/it/audiences/2009/documents/hf_ben-xvi_aud_20090826.html.

188 The "Charta oeacumenica," Strasbourg, April 22, 2001. Available at https://www.chiesavaldese.org/documents/charta_oecumen.pdf.

"common house" (*oikos*), the common house that is the Church where all Christians are summoned, and the common house of creation, the habitat provided by God's love for all people.

Thus, in 2002 John Paul II and Patriarch Bartholomew signed the "Venice Declaration" together, declaring their concern for the protection of the planet due to the social and ecological crisis, which brings violence, lack of resources, poverty, and disease. And they warn against the danger of technological and economic progress that does not recognize its limits before the integral good of humanity.

Today, Patriarch Bartholomew and Pope Francis continue this journey together, allowing themselves to be guided by the Holy Spirit, obedient to His directions, consistent with John's missionary mandate (John 13:35) to bear witness to Christ the Lord through mutual love, through a rediscovered and continually deepened fraternity, to work together against climate change, for the care of human beings and the earth.

Indeed, the Second Vatican Council speaks of ecumenism as an open path (cf. *Unitatis Redintegratio*, 24). The ecumenical journey is, indeed, a journey that the Churches make together and at the same time it is their own journey. This brings us back to Jesus' definition of Himself: "I am the Way, the Truth and the Life" (John 14:6).

On May 24, 2015, Pope Francis signed the Encyclical Letter *Laudato Si'* on the care of the common home. Nos. 7, 8 and 9 of the encyclical contain the thoughts of Patriarch Bartholomew;

actually, Pope Francis says that to prepare himself he read what the patriarch had written on the subject. This is a high point in the journey together of the Catholic Church and the Orthodox Church, which expresses coherence in recognizing the ecclesiality of the other Church, in assuming in its own Magisterium the teaching of the other Church.

Pope Francis, in fact, has stated that the deepening of faith in theological dialogue will be fruitful "only if it is done with an open mind and on one's knees. The theologian who rejoices in his complete and concluded thought is mediocre. The good theologian and philosopher has an open, that is, incomplete thought, always open to the *maius* of God and truth, always developing."[189] And on the eve of the feast of Saint Andrew, on November 29, 2014, Pope Francis bent down before Patriarch Bartholomew to receive his blessing.

When the patriarch was asked how he had received the inclusion of his thoughts in *Laudato Si'*, he replied by giving a glimpse of how normal this journey together with the pope has become for him too, of being in tune with each other and with the Word of God. He said that the kind reference made to him by the Pope did not surprise him because "whatever is true, whatever is

---

189 Cf. Pope Francis, "Discorso alla Comunità della Pontificia Università Gregoriana e ai Consociati del Pontificio Istituto Biblico e del Pontificio Istituto Orientale," April 10, 2014, *AAS* 106 (2014): 374. Cf. also *Costituzione Apostolica "Veritatis Gaudium" circa le Università e le Facoltà ecclesiastiche* (December 27, 2017), n. 3: the same passage is quoted.

honorable, whatever is just, whatever is pure, whatever is pleasing, whatever is commendable, if there is any excellence and if there is anything worthy of praise, think about these things" (Phil 4:8). And also because "all churches, all religions and disciplines confess the same truth, namely that the world is a divine gift, which we are all called to protect and preserve."[190]

On August 6, 2015, Pope Francis instituted the World Day of Prayer for the Care of Creation. In his letter of institution, he stated that he did so "sharing with [his] beloved brother Ecumenical Patriarch Bartholomew concerns for the future of creation" and accepting the suggestion of his representative, Metropolitan Ioannis of Pergamum, who had spoken at the presentation of *Laudato Si'*.[191] The choice of September 1 for this Day was in agreement with what "had been happening for some time in the Orthodox Church,"[192] the pope added, also hoping that the Day might also involve, in some way, other churches. In 2017, the message on the occasion of the Day of Prayer for the Care of Creation was co-signed for the first time by Pope Francis and Patriarch Bartholomew.

---

190 Andrea Tornielli, "Bartholomew: Curare l'ambiente è preoccuparsi anche della povertà," *LaStampa Vatican Insider*, June 19, 2019. Available at https://www.lastampa.it/vatican-insider/it/2015/06/19/news/bartolomeo-curare-l-ambiente-e-preoccuparsi-anche-della-poverta-1.35253311.
191 Pope Francis, *Lettera del Santo Padre Francesco per l'istituzione della "giornata mondiale di preghiera per la cura del creato" [1° settembre]*, August 6, 2015. Available at https://www.vatican.va/content/francesco/it/letters/2015/documents/papa-francesco_20150806_lettera-giornata-cura-creato.html.
192 Pope Francis, *Lettera*.

Since its beginning, the International Joint Commission for Dialogue between the Catholic Church and the Orthodox Church has published several documents mutually recognizing the common sacramental foundation of the Church. The most recent one is from 2016, and was signed in Chieti with the title "Synodality and Primacy during the First Millennium: Towards a Common Understanding in the Service of the Church's Unity."

In 2018, the International Theological Commission (ITC) also published a document: "Synodality in the Life and Mission of the Church." Thus, the centrality of the theme of synodality is becoming increasingly felt and gaining visibility.

The ITC document recognizes that it is a commitment for the Catholic faithful "to walk together with other Christians towards full and visible unity in the presence of the Crucified and Risen Lord: the only one able to heal the wounds inflicted on His Body throughout history and to reconcile differences according to the truth in love with the gift of the Spirit."[193]

The document recalls the conclusions reached by the Joint Commission of Orthodox Catholic Dialogue in Chieti[194] on synodality,

---

[193] International Theological Commission, "Synodality in the Life and Mission of the Church, March 2, 2018. Available at https://www.vatican.va/roman_curia/congregations/cfaith/cti_documents/rc_cti_20180302_sinodalita_en.html.

[194] Joint Commission of Orthodox Catholic Dialogue, *Sinodalità e primato nel primo millennio: verso una comune comprensione nel servizio all'unità della Chiesa*,

affirming, on the basis of Trinitarian faith, the development in the first millennium in both East and West of "structures of synodality inseparably linked with the primacy," whose theological and canonical heritage "constitutes the necessary reference ... to heal the wound of their division at the beginning of the third millennium."

We can say that so far in the relations between the Catholic Church and the Orthodox Church, despite the impasses suffered by the theological dialogue, the steps forward have been most important. This is undoubtedly due to the perseverance of the International Commission for Dialogue between the two Churches which, since 1980, has succeeded in reaching critical crossroads in the mutual understanding of crucial theological points. But it is also due to the farsightedness and tenacity of both Patriarch Bartholomew and Pope Francis, who continually strive to find ways and circumstances to affirm their desire and commitment to unity, to bring the faithful of the two Churches back to learning to be

---

Chieti, September 21, 2016. Available at http://www.christianunity.va/content/unitacristiani/it/dialoghi/sezione-orientale/chiese-ortodosse-di-tradizione-bizantina/commissione-mista-internazionale-per-il-dialogo-teologico-tra-la/documenti-di-dialogo/2016-sinodalita-e-primato-nel-primo-millennio--verso-una-comune-.html.

together again, to return to "breathing with both lungs,"[195] to get used to each other's presence and to mutual fraternity.[196]

The list of occasions on which Pope Francis and Patriarch Bartholomew have met in recent years has now become long, and it has become normal to see them together on occasions when Christian witness and common work become necessary for the good of humanity gripped by so many challenges and threats. It is an expression of the synodality between the Churches that is slowly being recovered.

In fact, Pope Francis, in his Apostolic Exhortation *Evangelii Gaudium* on the proclamation of the gospel in today's world, gives

---

195 Cf. Piero Coda, "Presentazione della Cattedra Ecumenica Internazionale Patriarca Athenagoras – Chiara Lubich: Le ragioni, la storia, le prospettive," in Gennadios Zervos and Piero Coda, *"Una porta aperta in Cielo": Una cattedra nel solco di Chiara Lubich e del Patriarca Athenagoras* (Figlini Incisa Valdarno: Istituto Universitario Sophia; Rome: Città Nuova 2022), 58. "Two lungs": the expression became famous with Pope John Paul II, who took it from the Russian poet, philosopher, and philologist Vjaceslav Ivanov (1866–1949), whom Nicolaj Berdiaev described as "the finest and most universal representative of 20th century Russian culture." Cf. also Piero Coda, "John Paul II and Chiara Lubich: Converging Development of the Dynamic Principles of Ecumenism in the Wake of Vatican II," *Melita theologica* 70, no. 1 (2020): 67–83. Cf. Yves Congar, *Diversità e comunione* (Assisi: Cittadella Editrice, 1983), 128 and note 17; the author notes: "We have often suggested this and repeatedly wished that the Church would breathe again with its two lungs." And in note 17 he refers to: "The 1952 conference published in *Chrétiens en dialogue*, 1966, p. 287 and then on various other occasions."
196 This is how one might interpret the various events mentioned in this paper and others, such as: the pilgrimage together to Jerusalem in 2014 on the occasion of the fiftieth anniversary of the one undertaken by Paul VI and Athenagoras, and their joint declaration on May 25; Bartholomew's participation in the Prayer Summit for Peace in the Vatican Gardens on June 9 2014; the journey together to the island of Lesbos in 2016 to visit refugees.

a concrete example of how the Catholic Church can learn from the Orthodox Church about fundamental aspects of the Church's life and experience: "To give but one example," says the pope, "in the dialogue with our Orthodox brothers and sisters, we Catholics have the opportunity to learn more about the meaning of episcopal collegiality and their experience of synodality" (EG, §246).

It is now customary to exchange visits between the See of Rome and the See of Constantinople on the patronal feasts of Saint Peter and Saint Andrew. Pope Francis, in his letter addressed to Patriarch Bartholomew on the feast of Saint Andrew on November 30, 2020, recalls the Ecumenical Patriarchate's commitment to ecumenism before the Catholic Church and the other churches. He quotes a passage from the Encyclical Letter issued by the Patriarchal Synod thirty years earlier, addressed to the churches around the world. It is a guardian of a truth of profound relevance for the direction of ecumenical dialogue: "When the different churches are inspired by love, and put it first in their judgement of others and in their relations with one another, they will be able, instead of increasing and widening existing disagreements, to attenuate and reduce them as much as possible."[197]

On October 7, 2021 at the Lateran University they together inaugurated the cycle of studies on Ecology and the Environment,

---

197 Pope Francis, "Message of Pope Francis to His Holiness Bartholomew I on the Occasion of the Feast of Saint Andrew," November 30, 2020. Available at https://www.vatican.va/content/francesco/en/messages/pont-messages/2020/documents/papa-francesco_20201130_messaggio-bartolomeo-i.html.

and in the afternoon of the same day they participated in the meeting promoted by the Community of Saint Egidio "All Peoples, Future Earth." On that occasion Pope Francis said: "[With Bartholomew] we share the duty to proclaim love for creation and the commitment to its custody," and revealed that while preparing the encyclical *Laudato Si'* "strong was the light that came from him and from the Church of Constantinople."[198] He went on to say that he had learnt and continued to learn a lot from the patriarch's reflection on the protection of creation. Regarding dialogue, the pope thanked the patriarch for his constant reminder of the need for this for achieving unity among Christians. While acknowledging that the journey will be long, he went on to say that "with God's help," it will certainly continue. And it will continue "together," because "the closeness and solidarity between our Churches are an indispensable contribution to universal brotherhood and social justice, which humanity so urgently needs."[199]

On the thirtieth anniversary of Bartholomew's election as Ecumenical Patriarch of Constantinople on October 22, 2021, Pope Francis wrote him a message[200] where he recalled and gave thanks

---

198 Pope Francis, "Atto accademico per l'istituzione del ciclo di studi sulla 'cura della nostra casa comune e tutela del creato' e della Cattedra Unesco 'on futures of education for sustainability,'" Address at the Pontifical Lateran University, Thursday, October 7, 2021. Available at https://www.vatican.va/content/francesco/it/speeches/2021/october/documents/20211007-istituzione-ciclostudi.html.
199 Pope Francis, "Atto accademico."
200 Tommaso Ciccoti, "Pope Francis Writes to Patriarch Bartholomew, *La Croix*, May 23, 2020. Available at https://international.la-croix.com/news/religion/pope-congratulates-bartholomew-on-30-years-as-ecumenical-patriarch/15095.

for the trajectory of a friendship that has been consolidating and deepening ever since. Francis recalls the day of his election to the Papacy, March 19, 2013, when the Patriarch unexpectedly went to Rome to greet his brother, something that had not happened since 1054. In this regard, it is with great honor that I can testify, from an interview granted to me by His Holiness Bartholomew, for a doctoral thesis, that he went to Rome for the inauguration of Pope Francis "spontaneously, with inspiration from above. Because," he said, "the work of unity is done by God through us: He gives us inspiration, illumination, orders, to do, to go, to visit . . . ." In his message for the feast of Saint Andrew, on November 30, 2021, Pope Francis, addressing his "beloved Brother in Christ," declared among other things his hope that, despite the various knots still to be untangled in the theological dialogue between the two Churches, Catholics and Orthodox can increasingly work together in those areas where it is not only possible to do so but even an imperative.[201]

Soon, in 2025, Christians will celebrate the 1700th anniversary of the Council of Nicaea that laid the first foundations of the Christian faith, and in the same year Catholics and Orthodox will celebrate Easter on the same date. These are occasions permeated with great significance and open possibilities to witness even more concretely and consistently to the mutual recognition gained so far in the

---

201   Cf. Pope Francis, "Message of Pope Francis to His Holiness Bartholomew I on the Occasion of the Feast of Saint Andrew," November 30, 2021. Available at https://www.vatican.va/content/francesco/it/messages/pont-messages/2021/documents/20211130-messaggio-bartolomeo.html.

consensus reached in theological dialogue. May the Holy Spirit continue to enlighten and inflame the hearts of all God's people with the desire for unity and inspire the next steps to be taken with courage and parity.

I conclude with a sentence from *Laudato Si'* that reaffirms not only the need to continue walking together but also how to walk: "Let us sing as we go. May our struggles and our concern for this planet never take away the joy of our hope" (§244).

IV. SOCIAL PERSPECTIVES

8. INTEGRAL ECOLOGY AND SOCIAL DOCTRINE: *FRATELLI TUTTI*

Giuseppe Argiolas

"Everything in the world is connected"[202] (LS, §16). This profound conviction constitutes one of the cornerstones on which Pope Francis' encyclical *Laudato Si'* rests, which, as he himself points out, is set out in such a way that, although each chapter "will have its own subject and specific approach, it will also take up and re-examine important questions previously dealt with" (LS, §16). The assertion "everything is connected, everything is related" is the natural premise for the concept of *integral ecology*.

What does it mean that everything is intimately connected? What are the connections involved? Why is this hermeneutic important for our work?

---

[202] Pope Francis, *Laudato Si'*, Encyclical letter on the care of our common home, May 24, 2015.

To fully understand this, we can read some passages from the apostolic exhortation *Evangelii Gaudium* where Pope Francis states:

> The whole is greater than the part, but it is also greater than the sum of its parts. There is no need, then, to be overly obsessed with limited and particular questions. We constantly have to broaden our horizons and see the greater good which will benefit us all. But this has to be done without evasion or uprooting. We need to sink our roots deeper into the fertile soil and history of our native place, which is a gift of God. We can work on a small scale, in our own neighborhood, but with a larger perspective. Nor do people who wholeheartedly enter into the life of a community need to lose their individualism or hide their identity; instead, they receive new impulses to personal growth. The global need not stifle, nor the particular prove barren.[203] (EG, §235)

And again,

> [The model] is the polyhedron, which reflects the convergence of all its parts, each of which preserves its distinctiveness. Pastoral and political activity alike seek to gather in this polyhedron the best of each. There is a place for the poor and their culture, their aspirations and their potential. Even people who can be considered dubious on account of their errors have something to offer which must not be overlooked. It is the convergence of peoples who, within the

---

[203] Pope Francis, *Evangelii Gaudium*, Apostolic exhortation on announcing the Gospel in today's world, November 24, 2013.

universal order, maintain their own individuality; it is the sum total of persons within a society which pursues the common good, which truly has a place for everyone. (EG 236)

This perspective, in my opinion, adequately accounts for the context in which we currently live: a reality characterized by systemic complexity,[204] in which the individual parts are interrelated by multilateral relations of interdependence, thanks to which they mutually influence each other in their way of being and becoming. Just think of globalization, the interconnection of economic and political systems on a planetary scale. But there is also the process of localization, with increasing attention being paid to highlighting its specificities. Today, we therefore speak of "Glocal," as the ability to bring together the global and the local.

The issue is relevant, its dimension is as big as the world: it is about the present and the future of our *common home*, the whole of creation. "As Christians, we are also called 'to accept the world as a sacrament of communion, as a way of sharing with God and our neighbors on a global scale'"[205] (LS, §9). In Saint Francis of Assisi "we see the extent to which concern for nature, justice towards the poor, commitment to society and inner peace are inseparable" (LS, §11).

Pope Francis introduces the concept of "integral ecology" here, stating that it "calls for openness to categories which transcend the

---

204 Edgar Morin, *La sfida della complessità*, new ed. (Florence: Editoriale Le Lettere, 2021).
205 Pope Francis, "Global Responsibility and Ecological Sustainability: Closing Remarks," I Halki Summit 1, Istanbul, June 20, 2012, quoted in *Laudato Si'*, §9.

language of mathematics and biology, and take us to the heart of what it is to be human" (LS, §11). Hence, "if we do not speak the language of fraternity and beauty in our relationship with the world, our attitude will be that of masters, consumers, ruthless exploiters, unable to set limits on their immediate needs. By contrast, if we feel intimately united with all that exists, then sobriety and care will well up spontaneously" (LS, §11).

"Today," Pope Francis continues, "however, we have to realize that a true ecological approach *always* becomes a social approach; it must integrate questions of justice in debates on the environment, so as to hear *both the cry of the earth and the cry of the poor*" (LS, §49).

A cry that has become, alas, increasingly polyphonic. Making us hear not only the piercing cry of those who have no work and no possessions, but also of those who, despite having all this, are oppressed by injustice, oppression, exploitation, instrumentalization: this is typical of both young people entering the world of work and mature adults who lose it, with a future that is, in their eyes, uncertain if not dark; the cry of those who experience the relational and existential poverty of a life lived without meaning; the cry of cultural poverty that prevents us from walking together.

> Certainly, we should be concerned lest other living beings be treated irresponsibly. But we should be particularly indignant at the enormous inequalities in our midst, whereby

we continue to tolerate some considering themselves more worthy than others. ... In practice, we continue to tolerate that some consider themselves more human than others, as if they had been born with greater rights. (LS, §90)

This is also well expressed in the words of Patriarch Bartholomew:

Economic development has not reduced the gap between rich and poor. Rather, it has established the priority of profit, at the expense of protecting the weak, and contributes to the exacerbation of environmental problems. And politics has become the servant of economics. Human rights and international law are elaborated and serve purposes unrelated to justice, freedom and peace. The refugee problem, terrorism, state violence, the humiliation of human dignity, modern forms of slavery and the Covid-19 epidemic are now confronting politics with new responsibilities and erasing its pragmatic logic.[206]

In fact, "Everything is connected. Concern for the environment thus needs to be joined to a sincere love for our fellow human beings and an unwavering commitment to resolving the problems of society" (LS, §91). "Moreover, when our hearts are authentically open to universal communion, this sense of fraternity excludes nothing and no one" (LS, §92). And therefore, "Peace, justice and the preservation of creation are three absolutely interconnected

---

206 Ecumenical Patriarch Bartholomew, "Bartolomeo su Fratelli Tutti: abbandoniamo indifferenza e cinismo," interview by Andrea Tornielli, Vatican News, October 20, 2020.

themes, which cannot be separated and treated individually without once again falling into reductionism."[207] "Everything is related, and we human beings are united as brothers and sisters on a wonderful pilgrimage, woven together by the love God has for each of His creatures and which also unites us in fond affection with brother sun, sister moon, brother river and mother earth" (LS, §92).

In this perspective Pope Francis identifies the elements of an "an *integral ecology*, one which clearly respects its human and social dimensions" (LS, §137):

I. Environmental, economic and social ecology (§138–142)
II. Cultural ecology (§143–146)
III. Ecology of daily life (§147–155)
IV. The principle of the common good (§156–158)
V. Justice between generations (§159–162)

The "social friendship" that Pope Francis proposes in *Fratelli Tutti* as a hermeneutical and action category starts from the principle that "unity is superior to conflict." The Pope writes, "This is not to opt for a kind of syncretism, or for the absorption of one into the other, but rather for a resolution which takes place on a higher plane and preserves what is valid and useful on both sides" (FT, §245). All of us know that "when we, as individuals and communities, learn to look beyond ourselves and our particular interests, then understanding and mutual commitment bear fruit ... in a setting where conflicts, tensions and even groups once considered inimical can attain a

---

207 Conference of Dominican Bishops, Pastoral Letter *Sobre la relación del hombre con la naturaleza* (January 21, 1987).

multifaceted unity that gives rise to new life"[208] (FT, §245).

Pope Francis also forcefully recalls the ecumenical dimension of the question:

> We ask God to strengthen unity in the Church, a unity enriched by diversities that are reconciled through the action of the Holy Spirit. For "we have been baptized by one Spirit into one body" (1 Cor 12:13), where each one makes his or her own distinctive contribution. As Saint Augustine said, "the ear sees through the eye, and the eye hears through the ear." It is also urgent that we continue to bear witness to a path of encounter between the different Christian denominations. We cannot forget the desire expressed by Jesus: that "all may be one" (John 17:21). Listening to his invitation, we acknowledge with sorrow that the process of globalization still lacks the prophetic and spiritual contribution of unity among all Christians. Nevertheless, "even as we make this journey towards full communion, we already have the duty to offer common witness to the love of God for all people by working together in the service of humanity."[209] (FT, §280)

This perspective spurs us to imagine broader scenarios, in the interreligious sphere, if it is true, as the Pope writes, that "we believers need to find occasions to speak with one another and

---

[208] Pope Francis, *Fratelli Tutti*. Encyclical letter on fraternity and social friendship, October 3, 2020.

[209] Common Declaration of Pope Francis and Ecumenical Patriarch Bartholomew, Jerusalem (May 25, 2014), 5, *L'Osservatore Romano* (May 26–27, 2014), p. 6.

to act together for the common good and the promotion of the poor" (FT, §282), it is also desirable to imagine that the fruit of this dialogue is openness to the whole of humanity. Indeed, as Patriarch Bartholomew points out,

> The Christians of the nascent Church called each other "brothers" .... For Christians, however, brothers are not only members of the Church, but all peoples. The Word of God took on human nature and united everything in itself. As all human beings are God's creation, so all have been included in the plan of salvation.[210]

What instrument exists to bring about this wish if not a Pact of Fraternity?

Pope Francis, in an audience granted to the Sophia University Institute, said:

> The pact is the keystone of creation and history, as the Word of God teaches us: the pact between God and man, the pact between generations, the pact between peoples and cultures, the pact—in the school—between teachers and students and also parents, the pact between humans, animals, plants and even the inanimate realities that make our common home beautiful and colorful. Everything is related to everything, everything is created to be a living icon of God who is a Trinity of Love! It is a priority task today, therefore, to educate to live this pact, indeed to be this pact alive in all these dimensions:

---

[210] Ecumenical Patriarch Bartholomew, "Bartolomeo su Fratelli Tutti."

to open the roads of the future to a new civilization that embraces humanity and the cosmos in universal fraternity. This vocation to fraternity, this living in brotherhood today is indispensable, we cannot continue without it.[211]

Going to the heart of the pact, we could identify "three natures" in it: a *dispositional* nature, a *factual* nature, and an experiential nature. The dispositional nature refers precisely to the disposition, to the explicit will to commit oneself to pursuing what is enshrined in the pact itself.[212] The factual nature, on the other hand, emphasizes the need for the commitment to be realized in actions consistent with what has been declared. In fact, if declarations are not transformed into actions, not only do they lose their meaning, but they even make the declarations themselves counterproductive and harmful. Finally, the experiential nature refers to feeling the effects of consistent behavior, the effects of lived solidarity,[213] in one's own skin. One could speak here of a true mysticism of the pact.

And what is the first "content," if we may say so, of the pact, if not fraternity? "In the name of the 'human brotherhood' that embraces all men, unites them and makes them equal," as the document on *human fraternity* (Abu Dhabi, February 4, 2019) states, it is possible to give the pact an ever new "form" "to cooperate with each other and to live as brothers/sisters who love each

---

211 Pope Francis, Address to the Comunità accademica dell'Istituto Universitario Sophia di Loppiano, Sala del Concistoro, November 14, 2019.
212 Cf. Giuseppe Argiolas, *Il valore dei valori: La governance nell'impresa socialmente orientata* (Rome: Città Nuova, 2014), 154.
213 Argiolas, *Il valore dei valori*, 154.

other."²¹⁴ This solid root allows the pact to be declined also in the city, also considering the duties, the responsibilities of religious communities towards the city.²¹⁵ It is thus possible to imagine different levels of the covenant intimately interconnected, but where fraternity, or rather the reciprocal love to live as brothers and sisters, stands as the "perspective horizon" of social life with the covenant declared, lived, experienced. It is a covenant of mutual love to be lived among brothers and sisters that projects us towards "universal communion" (FT, §95), of mercy to be received and given (FT, §59), of unity to be asked as a gift from God and with which to substantiate social bonds (FT, §287).

When Pope Francis on September 12, 2019[216] issued "the invitation to dialogue on the way we are building the future of the planet and the need to invest the talents of all, because every change needs an educational journey to bring to maturity a new universal solidarity and a more welcoming society," he grasped, I think, the sign of the times: to offer the new generations a "permanent education," an urgency of the present in order to "dream" the

---

214 Pope Francis and Grand Imam Ahmad Al-Tayeeb, "Document for World Peace and Living Together," Abu Dhabi, February 4, 2019.
215 Cf. Giuseppe Argiolas, "Quali doveri per le comunità religiose nella città?," presentation at the meeting of the Mediterraneo Frontiera di Pace, Incontro dei Vescovi e Sindaci del Mediterraneo, February 23–27, 2022.
216 Pope Francis, Message of His Holiness Pope Francis For the Launch of the Global Compact on Education, Vatican City, September 12, 2019.

future "with feet on the ground."²¹⁷ The educational challenge is at the center of Pope Francis' gaze, through it is in fact possible to build from the ground up the entire edifice of integral ecology to be developed in every dimension of social living in the *common home*: from economics to politics and international relations, from personal and social health to law, from art to communication and culture. Such an approach requires a precise gaze, capable of "discovering Christ in each human being, recognizing Him crucified in the sufferings of the abandoned and forgotten of our world, and risen in each brother or sister who makes a new start" (FT, §287).

It is He, Jesus Crucified and Risen, who is the Lord of history, and it is through Him, "the pupil of the eye of God,"[218] that we can look at our brothers and sisters and at history in order to enter into communion with God and communion among men and with the whole of creation. And we, the Lord's disciples, by our being in communion and in our ecclesial and social actions, are called to proclaim and testify that "God, in Christ, does not redeem only the individual person, but also the social relations between men."[219]

---

217 Argiolas, "Quali doveri per le comunità religiose nella città?," p. 4.
218 Cf. Gérard Rossé and Piero Coda, *Il grido d'abbandono: Scrittura, mistica, teologia* (Rome: Città Nuova, 2020).
219 Pontifical Council for Justice and Peace, *Compendium of the Social Doctrine of the Church*, §52; Pope Francis, Apostolic Exhortation *Evangelii Gaudium*, November 24, 2013, §178; cf. Second Vatican Council, *Lumen Gentium*, §9; cf. Congregation for the Doctrine of the Faith, Dicastery for Integral Human Development, "Œconomicæ et pecuniariæ quæstiones: Considerations for an ethical discernment about some aspects of the current economic-financial system," January 6, 2018, §4.

9. ORTHODOX AND ROMAN CATHOLIC SOCIAL PERSPECTIVES: COMPARING *FOR THE LIFE OF THE WORLD* WITH *FRATELLI TUTTI*

Vasilios N. Makrides

Introduction

In the contemporary global world which faces numerous challenges including environmental ones, it is extremely important that the Christian Churches offer their views publicly and develop their initiatives for sustaining the future of the planet together. Such a "collaboration" is not an empty promise, but has been systematically realized over the last decades through coordinated activities for the protection of the natural environment, currently between the Ecumenical Patriarch of Constantinople Bartholomew and Pope Francis. It is not accidental that both Church leaders have issued official encyclicals and texts on ecological issues, climate change, and the sustainability of planet Earth.[220] Given

---

220 See John Chryssavgis, *Bartholomew – Apostle and Visionary: 25 Years of*

that the Orthodox and Roman Catholic Churches have a long history of difficult and even thorny relations in the past, such recent rapprochements are more than welcome and continue to build stable bridges between the two Churches with far-reaching consequences in terms of promoting peace and solidarity, not only between them but also beyond the Church's confines.

Such common endeavors and the existence of commonalities between these two Churches should not, however, obfuscate the numerous differences that still exist between them on various levels, not least in the context of traditional Orthodox anti-Westernism and anti-Latinism.[221] This relates, among other things, to the degree of their world-relatedness, as well as to their relations with modernity respectively. Due to historical and other factors, the degree of world-relatedness (understood mainly in a neutral sense as denoting the Church's creative and generally positive entanglements with the world) has been stronger and more extensive in the Latin West than in the Orthodox East.[222] In addition, the encounter of

---

Guiding the Christian East, Foreword by Pope Francis (Nashville, TN: W Publishing Group, 2016); Pope Francis, *Our Mother Earth: A Christian Reading of the Challenge of the Environment*, with a Preface by Ecumenical Patriarch Bartholomew (Rome: Our Sunday Visitor, 2019).

221 See Thomas Bremer, "Der 'Westen' als Feindbild im theologisch-philosophischen Diskurs der Orthodoxie," in *Europäische Geschichte Online*, ed. Leibniz-Institut für Europäische Geschichte, Mainz, March 19, 2012 (URL: http://www.ieg-ego.eu/bremert-2012-de); Julia Anna Lis, *Antiwestliche Diskurse in der serbischen und griechischen Orthodoxie: Zur Konstruktion des "Westens" bei Nikolaj Velimirović, Justin Popović, Christos Yannaras und John S. Romanides* (Berlin: Peter Lang, 2019).

222 See Vasilios N. Makrides, "Secularity and Christianity: Comparing Orthodox

Roman Catholicism with modernity has been a quite painful one historically, yet after the Second Vatican Council (1962–1965) a significant breakthrough took place that marked a new era for this Church in many domains.[223] More importantly, the intensification of the "Social Question" since the nineteenth century forced the Roman Catholic Church to show a greater interest in social problems and issues. This resulted, among other things, in the long tradition of related social encyclicals that has continued to this day, starting with *Rerum Novarum* (1891) by Pope Leo XIII.[224] Not accidentally, the current Pope Francis has also issued two such social encyclicals, namely *Laudato Si'* ("Praise Be to You")[225] in 2015 and *Fratelli Tutti* ("All Brothers")[226] in 2020, which exhibit numerous conceptual connections and continuities (e.g., in terms of the close interrelation between the humans and the natural world[227]). This continuing long

---

with Western Perspectives," *The Greek Orthodox Theological Review* 63, no. 3–4 (2018 [2021]): 49–107. See also idem, "Christian Communities, Civil Society and Civic Engagement in East and West: Convergences and Divergences," in Rupert Graf Strachwitz, ed., *Religious Communities and Civil Society in Europe: Analyses and Perspectives on a Complex Interplay*, vol. 2 (Berlin: Oldenbourg, 2020), 239–285.

223 See, among others, Catherine E. Clifford and Massimo Faggioli, eds., *The Oxford Handbook of Vatican II* (Oxford: Oxford University Press, 2022); Richard R. Gaillardetz, "Synodality and the Francis Pontificate: A Fresh Reception of Vatican II," *Theological Studies* 84 (2023): 44–60.

224 See David J. O'Brien and Thomas Anthony Shannon, eds., *Catholic Social Thought: Encyclicals and Documents from Pope Leo XIII to Pope Francis*, 3rd revised edition (Maryknoll, NY: Orbis, 2016).

225 https://www.vatican.va/content/francesco/en/encyclicals/documents/papa-francesco_20150524_enciclica-laudato-si.html.

226 https://www.vatican.va/content/francesco/en/encyclicals/documents/papa-francesco_20201003_enciclica-fratelli-tutti.html.

227 See Jelson Roberto de Oliveira and Clovis Ultramari, "The Eutopian City: The

tradition means that "Social Doctrine" within Roman Catholicism has developed into a full scholarly and academic discipline through an extensive theoretical elaboration, a systematic articulation, and numerous innovative contributions, such as regarding the concepts of subsidiarity, human dignity, solidarity, common good, charity, distributism, and social justice.[228] There were further repercussions of such social inquiries and initiatives historically, such as in the domain of politics through the foundation of Christian Democratic parties and other political movements around the globe. The public presentation of such comprehensive social documents is hardly a rarity in the Catholic world—consider, for example, the *Compendium of the Social Doctrine of the Church*, issued in 2004 by the Pontifical Council for Justice and Peace during the Pontificate of Pope John Paul II.[229] There are constant cross-references between these official documents and encyclicals, showing that the Catholic social teaching has developed during all these years and has tried to grasp the spirit of the changing times by actualizing itself accordingly. Quite important here was the continuous dialogue of Catholic social thinkers with various scholarly disciplines (e.g., social sciences, economics, philosophy in their secular versions), a

---

Challenge of Urban Conviviality in the *Laudato Si'* and *Fratelli Tutti* Encyclicals," *International Journal of Public Theology* 16, no. 2 (2022): 154–173.

228 See Charles E. Curran, *Catholic Social Teaching, 1891–Present: A Historical, Theological, and Ethical Analysis* (Washington, DC: Georgetown University Press, 2002); Daniel Schwindt, *Catholic Social Teaching: A New Synthesis (*Rerum Novarum *to* Laudato Si'*)* (McPherson, KS: Agnus Dei, 2015).

229 https://www.vatican.va/roman_curia/pontifical_councils/justpeace/documents/rc_pc_justpeace_ doc_20060526_compendio-dott-soc_en.html.

fact that resulted in a philosophical-natural law and human dignity-based argumentation. All this has also led to the establishment, dissemination, and institutionalization of related activities, such as through the founding of university schools, specialized chairs, research centers, and head offices, as well as through numerous publications. Suffice to mention the "Laudato Si' Research Institute" (Campion Hall, University of Oxford), established in 2019, which conducts cutting-edge multidisciplinary research for societal transformation on the most pressing ecological and social issues of today. In this context, the notion of "integral ecology" is quite important, especially as elaborated in the encyclical *Laudato Si'*, which points to the close interdependence between social and environmental issues on the planet. These are not considered as separate parts of various crises, but as one complex and multi-layered deep crisis that demands an integral perspective to thoroughly understand and practically handle this situation, by drawing on systematic research across numerous engaged scholarly disciplines that had worked mostly in isolation in the past.[230]

Compared with such an established Roman Catholic tradition regarding social concerns and issues, the corresponding situation in the Orthodox East has been quite different. Historically, otherworldly and unworldly trends and orientations have often taken the lead and predominated.[231] As such, they have left their

---

230 https://lsri.campion.ox.ac.uk/.
231 See Demosthenes Savramis, "Max Webers Beitrag zum besseren Verständnis der ostkirchlichen 'außerweltlichen' Askese," *Kölner Zeitschrift für Soziologie und*

imprint on Eastern Orthodox societies, manifesting a weak world affirmation and more specifically a weak engagement with social issues in terms of articulating a systematic social teaching on the basis of modern developments.[232] Usually, such issues have been examined from the perspective of the past Orthodox tradition; for instance, with reference to the normative authority of the Church Fathers, whose views have been regarded as transhistorically valid and of perennial significance. Yet, this orientation has not enabled fresh, innovative, and updated thinking on social issues beyond the past tradition. In addition, there has been neglect in formalizing Orthodox positions on social issues, such that the Orthodox side has not offered much beyond some concise statements and reports in this specific domain. Hence, if one were to search for an official and normative Orthodox position on a specific social issue, one would have a difficult time locating it within this very nebulous framework. The internal fragmentation of the entire Orthodox world also contributed to this deficit. On top of this, there has often been critique of the Roman Catholic and Protestant trajectories on social issues, which have not been deemed worthy of emulation, given that they allegedly led to additional problems and complications (e.g., the increased worldliness and secularization of the Church

---

Sozialpsychologie (Sonderheft) 7 (1963): 334–358.

232   See Vasilios N. Makrides, "Why Does the Orthodox Church Lack Systematic Social Teaching?," *Skepsis. A Journal for Philosophy and Interdisciplinary Research* 23 (2013): 281–312. See also idem, "Die soziale Verantwortung in der Sicht der Orthodoxen Kirche," in Anton Rauscher et al., eds., *Handbuch der Katholischen Soziallehre* (Berlin: Duncker & Humblot, 2008), 249–254.

in the West). The lack of a systematic approach to Orthodox social ethics had been regarded neither as a deficit nor as problematic.[233] The Orthodox have had no need of a systematic social doctrine—so the argument goes; instead they have had a sufficient "social ethos" that can provide necessary guidelines and answers in a context of freedom. To use the expression of a well-known Orthodox theologian, Georges Florovsky: "For Orthodox Christians there is no such thing as Christian Ethics."[234] In such cases, there has also been an urgently felt need to demarcate the Orthodox side from "fallen" Western Christianity, which has had many negative consequences for the Orthodox side, such as ideologizations, distortions, and a-historical projections. As a result, traditionalism, mysticism, and nationalism have often functioned as outlets for Orthodox social inquiries. All this does not, however, signify that the Orthodox have not dealt with social problems in practical terms, given that philanthropic activities have always been a top priority in a variety of forms. Orthodox social ideas have often been expressed through acts of philanthropy, charitable works, and efforts to promote social harmony and well-being.[235] At the same time, the Orthodox side has always tried to keep its distance from Western Christianity and has been critical of the enhanced social activism of the latter as being

---

233 See Vigen Guroian, "Notes Toward an Eastern Orthodox Ethic," *The Journal of Religious Ethics* 9, no. 2 (1981): 228–244, at 240.
234 Cited in Thomas Hopko, "Orthodox Christianity and Ethics," in *1995 Orthodox Education Day Book* (Crestwood, NY: St Vladimir's Seminary Press, 1995), 6–7, at 6.
235 See Matthew J. Pereira, ed., *Philanthropy and Social Compassion in the Eastern Orthodox Tradition* (New York: Theotokos, 2010).

detrimental to the true eschatological character of the Christian religion.[236]

Such widespread views in the Orthodox world were seriously tested in the wake of the radical changes in the former Eastern Bloc (1989–1991) and the ongoing globalization at the turn of the twenty-first century, which brought about many unprecedented challenges and new contestations. This led to certain concrete actions, such as the systematic ones by the Ecumenical Patriarchate of Constantinople under Patriarch Bartholomew for the protection of the environment,[237] which drew huge attention and praise on a global scale.[238] In fact, under his leadership, the Patriarchate of Constantinople has developed into a modern global player of

---

236 See John Meyendorff, "The Christian Gospel and Social Responsibility: The Eastern Orthodox Tradition in History," in Frank Forrester Church and Timothy Francis George, eds., *Continuity and Discontinuity in Church History: Essays Presented to George Huntston Williams on the Occasion of His 65th Birthday* (Leiden: Brill, 1979), 118–130; Razvan Porumb, "Orthodoxy in Engagement with the 'Outer' World: The Dynamic of the 'Inward-Outward' Cycle," *MDPI Religions* 2017, no. 8 (2018): 131 (doi: 10.3390/rel8080131).

237 See, among others, John Chryssavgis, "Ecumenical Patriarch Bartholomew: Insights into an Orthodox Christian Worldview," *International Journal of Environmental Studies* 64 (2007): 9–18; John Chryssavgis, ed., *Cosmic Grace, Humble Prayer. The Ecological Vision of the Green Patriarch Bartholomew* (Grand Rapids, MI: Eerdmans, 2009); Ecumenical Patriarch Bartholomew, *On Earth as in Heaven: Ecological Vision and Initiatives of Ecumenical Patriarch Bartholomew*, ed. John Chryssavgis (New York: Fordham University Press, 2012).

238 See Ecumenical Patriarch Bartholomew, *In the World, Yet Not of the World: Social and Global Initiatives of Ecumenical Patriarch Bartholomew*, ed. John Chryssavgis (New York: Fordham University Press, 2010); Krzysztof Lesniewski, "Ecumenical Patriarch Bartholomew's 'Green Message' to the World," *Roczniki Teologii Ekumenicznej* 3, no. 58 (2011): 33–48.

great influence and importance.[239] It is also no wonder that some Orthodox Churches began to reconsider their position on social issues. The Russian Orthodox Church was the first to do so by issuing an official document in 2000 titled "Bases of the Social Concept"[240] and further documents later (e.g., on Human Dignity, Freedom, and Rights in 2008).[241] This was a Church that had emerged from a highly negative experience of communism in the twentieth century and intended to make a new beginning by officially systematizing and

---

239   See John Chryssavgis, ed., *Global Initiatives of Ecumenical Patriarch Bartholomew: Peace, Reconciliation, and Care for Creation* (Notre Dame, IN: University of Notre Dame Press, 2023); Ioannis N. Grigoriadis, "The Ecumenical Patriarchate as a Global Actor: Between the End of the Cold War and the Ukrainian Ecclesiastical Crisis," *The Journal of the Middle East and Africa* 13, no. 3 (2022): 345–358. See also Paschalis Kitromilides, *Religion and Politics in the Orthodox World: The Ecumenical Patriarchate and the Challenges of Modernity* (London: Routledge, Taylor and Francis, 2019).

240   See Josef Thesing and Rudolf Uertz, eds., *Die Grundlagen der Sozialdoktrin der Russisch-Orthodoxen Kirche* (Sankt Augustin: Konrad-Adenauer-Stiftung, 2001); Alexander Agadjanian, "Breakthrough to Modernity, Apologia for Traditionalism: The Russian Orthodox View of Society and Culture in Comparative Perspective," *Religion, State & Society* 31 (2003): 327–346; Regina Elsner, "20 Jahre nach der Veröffentlichung der 'Sozialkonzeption' der Russischen Orthodoxen Kirche. Bleibende Leerstelle zwischen Moral und Politik," *Jahrbuch für Christliche Sozialwissenschaften* 61 (2020): 213–234.

241   See Alfons Brüning and Evert van der Zweerde, eds., *Orthodox Christianity and Human Rights* (Leuven: Peeters, 2012); Vasilios N. Makrides, "Die Menschenrechte aus orthodox-christlicher Sicht: Evaluierung, Positionen und Reaktionen," in Mariano Delgado, Volker Leppin, and David Neuhold, eds., *Schwierige Toleranz: Der Umgang mit Andersdenkenden und Andersgläubigen in der Christentumsgeschichte* (Fribourg/Stuttgart: Academic Press/ Kohlhammer, 2012), 293–320; Kristina Stoeckl, *The Russian Orthodox Church and Human Rights* (London: Routledge, 2014); Vasilios N. Makrides, Jennifer Wasmuth, and Stefan Kube, eds., *Christentum und Menschenrechte in Europa: Perspektiven und Debatten in Ost und West* (Frankfurt am Main: Peter Lang, 2016).

publicly presenting its views on various social issues. Yet, its overall orientation was rather defensive, if not negative, towards secular, liberal modernity, while exhibiting a clear anti-Western attitude. This notwithstanding, it was the first step that an Orthodox Church had ever taken in such a direction, which was certainly a worthwhile and commendable development.[242]

In the following years, Orthodox awareness of social problems appeared to become stronger, especially in view of formulating a more unified position on such issues from a pan-Orthodox perspective. The Holy and Great Council of the Orthodox Church (Crete 2016) did produce a short document about the mission of the Church in the modern world,[243] yet it faced serious internal problems due to the non-participation of four Orthodox Churches (especially the Moscow Patriarchate) in the synod. It also postponed the most serious and extensive dealings with such issues to a future council. However, soon after the Crete Council, things went very quickly. An Orthodox theological commission was entrusted with the task of formulating a new social document under the aegis of

---

242 See Regina Elsner, *Die Russische Orthodoxe Kirche vor der Herausforderung Moderne: Historische Wegmarken und theologische Optionen im Spannungsfeld von Einheit und Vielfalt* (Würzburg: Echter, 2018).

243 See Vasilios N. Makrides, "Le concile panorthodoxe de 2016: Quelques réflexions sur les défis auxquels le monde orthodoxe doit faire face," *Istina* 62 (2017): 5–26; idem, "Zwischen Tradition und Erneuerung: Das Panorthodoxe Konzil 2016 angesichts der modernen Welt," *Catholica. Vierteljahresschrift für ökumenische Forschung* 71 (2017): 18–32. See also Vasilios N. Makrides and Sebastian Rimestad, eds., *The Pan-Orthodox Council of 2016: A New Era for the Orthodox Church? Interdisciplinary Perspectives* (Berlin: Peter Lang, 2021).

the Ecumenical Patriarchate. The result was the formulation of *For the Life of the World: Toward a Social Ethos of the Orthodox Church* in early 2020. In character, it was more open and pluralist towards the modern world and the global challenges than the Russian Orthodox documents, since it tried to address them critically, yet constructively. It was also not regarded as a final document, but as a first one on the way to acquiring pan-Orthodox recognition, validity, and acceptance. A look at the drafting theological commission reveals that most of its members came from the so-called "Orthodox diaspora" (mainly from the USA) including even some converts to Orthodoxy. This was a novel phenomenon in the Orthodox world that attested to the emergence of an "Orthodox Christian cosmopolitanism"[244] with a great potential in the future for transforming the Orthodox world through a necessary *aggiornamento*.

Needless to say, these developments were very positively received by the Western Churches, especially concerning their significance for inter-Christian exchange and cooperation on social issues. More specifically with regard to Orthodox–Catholic relations: The above developments within the Orthodox world, together with the increased exchange and cooperation between the two Churches on an official level in the last decades, show that

---

244 See Vasilios N. Makrides, "Ὁ ἀναδυόμενος «Ὀρθόδοξος κοσμοπολιτισμός»: Τό νέο ἐπίσημο κείμενο γιά τό κοινωνικό ἦθος τῆς Ὀρθόδοξης Ἐκκλησίας καί ἡ σημασία του," Σύναξη 162 (April–June 2022): 75–81; idem, "Ὀρθόδοξος Χριστιανικός Κοσμοπολιτισμός: Ἡ ἀνάδυση ἑνός νέου φαινομένου στόν Ὀρθόδοξο κόσμο καί ἡ σημασία του," Ἀχιλλίου Πόλις 9 (2023): 447–482.

there is a clear rapprochement between them that needs further examination, consideration, and assessment. For this reason, one appropriate way to proceed would be to look more closely at various official social documents of the two Churches in order to locate both common trajectories and potential differences and to assess their importance in view of the current global challenges.

For the Life of the World and *Fratelli Tutti*:
A Comparative Overview

To this purpose, it would be interesting to take a brief comparative look at two documents that both appeared in 2020 trying to offer guidance on social and ethical issues of our time: the Orthodox *For the Life of the World: Toward a Social Ethos of the Orthodox Church* (henceforth FLOW) on March 27 under the aegis of the Ecumenical Patriarchate of Constantinople[245] and the previously mentioned Catholic encyclical *Fratelli Tutti* (henceforth FT) on October 3 by Pope Francis.[246] On the one hand, the Orthodox document attempted a more comprehensive formulation of a related social teaching—somewhat differently than the aforementioned Russian Orthodox one—and hence touched upon a large variety of issues, ranging

---

245 https://www.goarch.org/-/life-of-the-world-thurs. See also David Bentley Hart and John Chryssavgis, eds., *For the Life of the World: Toward a Social Ethos of the Orthodox Church* (Brookline, MA: Holy Cross Orthodox Press, 2020).

246 On this encyclical, see, among others, Marcus Mescher, *The Study Guide to the Encyclical Letter of Pope Francis: Fratelli Tutti, on Fraternity and Social Friendship* (Mahwah, NJ: Paulist, 2021); Ursula Nothelle-Wildfeuer and Lukas Schmitt, eds., *Unter Geschwistern? Die Sozialenzyklika Fratelli tutti: Perspektiven – Konsequenzen – Kontroversen* (München: Herder, 2021).

from children's issues, climate change, democracy, disability, and human rights to marriage, pluralism, sexuality, violence, and women's issues—to mention but a few.[247] On the other hand, the Catholic document was far more specific in its scope, as it was also related, among other things, to the unexpected eruption of the global epidemiological crisis of Covid-19 and its immense consequences (§7, 32–36, 54, 168), considering that this pandemic has abruptly and radically changed the entire world. Aside from its specific traits, FT is part of the long, multifaceted, and established tradition of Catholic social documents that looks back on a history of more than one hundred years. Opinions also vary regarding which specific Catholic and Orthodox documents may be appropriately compared with one another. It has been argued, for example, that FLOW "is not so much a presentation of social ethics, as a treatise on moral theology comprehensively considered. The nearest Roman Catholic parallel would be *Veritatis Splendor*, rather than one of the social encyclicals."[248] This notwithstanding, both FLOW and FT clearly have a lot in common that allows for a comparison.

---

247 On this document, see the monograph by Dietmar Schon, *Berufen zur Verwandlung der Welt: Die Orthodoxe Kirche in sozialer und ethischer Verantwortung* (Regensburg: Friedrich Pustet, 2021). See also the special thematic journal issues devoted to it: *Religion & Gesellschaft in Ost und West (RGOW)*, Vol. 48, Issue 11 (2020); *Ecumenical Trends*, Vol. 49, Issue 5 (2020); Σύναξη. Τριμηνιαία Ἔκδοση Σπουδῆς στὴν Ὀρθοδοξία 162 (April–June 2022); *Istina*, Vol. 65, Issue 4 (2020); *Review of Ecumenical Studies – RES (Sibiu)*, Vol. 13, Issue 1 (2021); *Studies in Christian Ethics*, Vol. 35, Issue 2 (2022); *Theology Today*, Vol. 78, Issue 4 (2022).
248 Jean Porter, "*For the Life of the World:* Some Reflections," *Theology Today* 78, no. 4 (2022): 357–364, at 358.

For example, they both support an integral view of God's creation and its necessary protection through the crafting of an ecological spirituality with direct practical consequences.

Starting with FT, it places particular emphasis upon the significance of fraternity, social friendship, and solidarity among humans for enabling a better, more just, peaceful, and equitable world and for addressing pressing global challenges. This is due to the growing awareness that the current and future global problems and challenges, and in general the effects of the ongoing globalization process (e.g., war and armed conflicts, poverty and social inequalities, migration, climate change, environmental degradation), cannot be faced in isolation and fragmentation by humans worldwide, but only as a "community of belonging and solidarity" (§36); namely, in coordination, cooperation, and mutual understanding for the common good. Individual action and initiatives are still deemed necessary, yet the principal conviction is that global difficulties and complications ask precisely for concerted and coordinated global action. In terms of concrete measures for action, FT stresses the need to establish civil institutions and mechanisms towards a better and more genuine international cooperation (§108, 165, 172). It goes without saying that this fraternal appeal to a "shared humanity" (§60) and a "shared responsibility for the development of the world" (§162) aims at overcoming ethnic/national, religious, cultural, linguistic, political, and other divisions, which have brought a great deal of harm to humanity and the environment in the past. Promoting a new humanism of global outreach and significance, FT recognizes the dignity and rights of every person, irrespective of their background, race, religion, or social status (§86). Peace, reconciliation, and social harmony are considered as absolutely necessary in a world often marked by aggravated divisions and prolonged conflicts. The document calls for dialogue, negotiation, and peaceful resolution of conflicts while highlighting the importance of forgiveness and the potential for reconciliation (§240, 271, 279).

Additionally, this appeal to "universal fraternity" is given a theological legitimation through presenting humans as co-responsible in enabling a better world, thus contributing to the preservation of God's creation. The same applies to the various categories of suffering, afflicted, and discriminated people due to all kinds of troubles and evils, who need immediate support in order to be integrated in society (§97–98). Within such a fraternal framework, every Christian is able to recognize Jesus Christ in the face of such tormented persons and make his/her contribution accordingly. In an era of extreme individualism and corresponding lifestyles, it is deemed necessary to develop a stronger communal ideal and to go outside one's own self, seeking the fulfilment of human existence in the fraternal encounter with other human beings and a mutual understanding. More specifically, due to the global problem of human migration, which appeared in a pressing form during the "refugee crisis" of 2015, FT touches upon the issue of "locals" and "foreigners" by blurring the distinction between them (§37–41). If, for instance, needy people are on the move from one place to another, they also have certain "rights" to the goods of the host territory, which should not be considered as the "exclusive" property of the native residents (§124–127). Such a stance signifies a major critique of the predominant cultures of individualism and consumerism that prioritize self-interest and material possessions over the common good and global solidarity (§128–132). In FT, which clearly promotes the virtue of sharing, the perfect model for such a universal fraternity is found in the biblical parable of the Good Samaritan, in which Jesus Christ's charity becomes archetypical for universal fraternity and social friendship (§62, 66–67, 69, 71, 79-80, 101, 165). Examples from Catholic history are also mentioned, such as that of the beatified French priest Charles de Foucauld (1858–1916) and his ideal of a total surrender to God towards an identification with the poor in the depths of the African desert.[249] The same is also true for non-Catholic exemplary figures like Martin Luther King, Desmond Tutu, and Mahatma Gandhi, who are also portrayed as examples to be imitated (§286–287). In addition, FT also directs its critique against populist and nationalist ideologies that appear to be on the rise worldwide, promoting xenophobic and exclusionary attitudes (§11, 46, 156–162, 181). In contrast, the Christian and more general ideal is to build future societies that embrace diversity and foster inclusion.

---

[249] See Brunetto Salvarani, *Fino a farsi fratello di tutti: Charles de Foucauld e papa Francesco*, (Assisi: Cittadella Editrice, 2022).

Furthermore, the fraternal ideal in FT is not only limited to humans, but also pertains to the whole of creation with tangible, practical consequences for the environment. As a result, the encyclical repeatedly emphasizes the need for an "integral human development" in a holistic way that will offer a new understanding of global challenges and concomitant solutions (§21, 112, 133, 169, 235, 257, 276). It thus turns openly against the individualistic indifference towards global challenges often observed today, including limitless consumption, the trend to wastefulness, lack of concern for the environment, and the emergence of a throwaway culture (§13, 35, 36, 44, 125, 222). These attitudes are considered as resulting from the uncontrollable development of the market economy and its immense automatization in the global age, a development that has clear detrimental effects upon society (§33, 109, 122, 168). This is because such stances utterly disregard the needs and hopes of the most vulnerable members of society. As is to be expected, the outspoken call is for a more equitable distribution of resources and opportunities in global terms (§129-130). In general, FT should be considered in the context of previous encyclicals of Pope Francis, such as *Evangelii Gaudium* ("The Joy of the Gospel") of 2013 and the aforementioned *Laudato Si'*, which also dealt with similar issues with the aim of enabling a more compassionate world and more inclusive societies.

Turning now to FLOW, aside from its broader scope, it also focuses on social justice and the importance of promoting the common good through human solidarity, peace, and reconciliation. It clearly recognizes the sanctity of life and the dignity of every human person, created in the image and likeness of God, regardless of background or socio-political circumstances (§24). Unequivocally, this document affirms the fundamental unity of all human beings. It highlights the Church's commitment to engaging with the world and addressing societal challenges and urges Orthodox Christians to actively participate in the transformation of society. It stresses the need for the Church to defend and promote human rights, including the rights of the poor, marginalized, and vulnerable (§34). Hence, numerous related issues are discussed from a communitarian perspective: "[God's love] calls us to an ever greater communion with one another, with all those whose lives we touch, with the fullness of creation, and thus with him who is the creator of all" (§3). This is not surprising, given that Orthodox theology has traditionally emphasized the fundamental aspects of communion, love, and interrelatedness between the Trinitarian God, humanity, and the whole of the creation (especially through the doctrine of God's Incarnation in the person of Jesus Christ).[250] Influential theological currents in the Orthodox world, such as personalism, have put particular emphasis on this dimension, which is regarded as the opposite of the fragmentation of human beings and the

---

[250] See Guroian, "Notes," 232–234; Costa Carras, "The Holy Trinity, the Church and Politics in a Secular World," in Andrew Walker and Costa Carras, eds., *Living Orthodoxy in the Modern World: Orthodox Christianity and Society* (Crestwood, NY: St. Vladimir's Seminary Press, 2000), 189–216.

world characterizing the modern age.[251] It goes without saying that such an Orthodox communitarian framework also has an impact on the development of an Orthodox ecological theology, which has indeed flourished in the last decades as a counter to the ongoing ecological degradation of the world[252]—a topic that is also touched upon in the document (§2, 76).

Perhaps more importantly, FLOW tries to ground its social vision in a eucharistic and Trinitarian theology of interpersonal relations that may potentially lead to an overcoming of egocentrism through the promotion of a communitarian lifestyle. Social ethics and the solution of social problems acquire thereby a strong sacramental dimension, which again belongs to the main features of an Orthodox view of the world and clearly reveals the experiential character of Orthodox theology.[253] The Eucharist, being the source and summit

---

251   See Aristotle Papanikolaou, "Personhood and Its Exponents in Twentieth-Century Orthodox Theology," in Mary B. Cunningham and Elizabeth Theokritoff, eds., *The Cambridge Companion to Orthodox Christian Theology* (Cambridge: Cambridge University Press, 2008), 232–245; Alexis Torrance and Symeon Paschalidis, eds., *Personalism in the Byzantine Christian Tradition: Early, Medieval, and Modern Perspectives* (Abingdon: Routledge, 2018).

252   From the very rich literature on the topic, see Alexander Belopopsky and Dimitri Oikonomou, eds., *Orthodoxy and Ecology: Resource Book* (Bialystok: Syndesmos, 1996); Tamara Grdzelidze, "Creation and Ecology: How Does the Orthodox Church Respond to Ecological Problems?," *The Ecumenical Review* 54, no. 3 (2002): 211–218; John Chryssavgis and Bruce Foltz, eds., *Toward an Ecology of Transfiguration: Orthodox Christian Perspectives on Environment, Nature and Creation* (New York: Fordham University Press, 2013); Theodota Nantsou and Nikolaos Asproulis, eds., *The Orthodox Church Addresses the Climate Crisis* (Athens/Volos: Volos Academy Publications, 2021).

253   See Stefanos Athanasiou, "Asketische und liturgische Erfahrung als Grundlage des Sozialethos," *Religion & Gesellschaft in Ost und West (RGOW)* 48, no. 11

of the Church's life and mission, is considered to have indeed a transformative power in shaping an Orthodox social ethos (§1–2, 5, 8). This is because eucharistic spirituality is believed to foster solidarity, compassion, and stewardship of creation.[254] Hence, FLOW encourages the Orthodox faithful to live out their faith in their relationships, families, workplaces, and communities, bringing the values of the Kingdom of God to bear on social, economic, and political structures (§§52, 73, 78, 79). In connection to this, worth mentioning is also the strong eschatological character of the document (§79–80), not the least considering that eschatology has always occupied a pivotal role in Orthodox theology and specifically in ethics and soteriology.[255] In other words, the Church looks at the world and at creation from the perspective of the coming Kingdom of God. This implies a perspective of humility and asceticism towards the world as an effective counter-measure against the abundance of human overconfidence and consumerist spirit. In addition, this perspective is closely connected with the ideal of deification

---

(November 2020): 3–5.
254 See Vigen Guroian, "Seeing Worship as Ethics: An Orthodox Perspective," *The Journal of Religious Ethics* 13, no. 2 (1985): 332–359; John D. Zizioulas, *The Eucharistic Communion and the World* (London: T & T Clark, 2011); John Chryssavgis, *Creation as Sacrament: Reflections on Ecology and Spirituality* (London: T&T Clark, 2019); John Chryssavgis and Nikolaos Asproulis, eds., *Priests of Creation: John Zizioulas on Discerning an Ecological Ethos* (London: T&T Clark, 2021).
255 See Guroian, "Notes," 231, 236–240.

(*theosis*, θέωσις), which is equally central in Orthodox theology[256] and has implications for the entire creation as well (§3, 15, 20, 31).

No doubt, it is obvious from this concise presentation of the two documents that there are several common themes between them regarding the articulation of a Christian identity in the current global age and the multifaceted social-ethical role Christians may undertake in the world. Thus, I would like to single out three particular elements of broader significance that are addressed in both documents, although not exactly in the same way:

First, the idea of the *global interconnectedness* of issues in the broadest possible sense (e.g., environmental, economic, political, social, cultural, ethical), underlining the importance of this integral perspective for the sake of the planet. This is closely related to the concept of "integral ecology," which was amply expounded and theologically grounded in the previous encyclical *Laudato Si'*[257] and which is also present in the ecological vision of Patriarch Bartholomew.[258] It is about the fundamental idea that everything is connected and closely related at every possible level in the world in which humans live, at the intersections between the natural

---

256 See Guroian, "Notes," 229–230.
257 See Matthew Eaton, Dennis O'Hara, and Michael T. Ross, eds., *Integral Ecology for a More Sustainable World: Dialogues with* Laudato Si' (Lanham, MD: Lexington, 2019).
258 See Maria G. Sereti, "The Contribution of Ecumenical Patriarch Bartholomew to the Configuration of an Ecumenical 'Integral Ecology,'" *The Ecumenical Review* 70, no. 4 (2018): 617–626.

and the social systems. The question is, hence, how to change concepts and attitudes that create both environmental crises and socio-economic inequalities and how to think of comprehensive solutions. In FT, this global interrelationship is mainly considered necessary on the level of creating a universal fraternity, fraternal love, social friendship, and solidarity. Explicit reference is here made to the global challenge of the Covid-19 pandemic, "exposing our false securities. Aside from the different ways that various countries responded to the crisis, their inability to work together became quite evident. For all our hyper-connectivity, we witnessed a fragmentation that made it more difficult to resolve problems that affect us all" (§7). This is because "to care for the world in which we live means to care for ourselves" (§17). The hope was that "God willing, after all this, we will think no longer in terms of 'them' and 'those,' but only 'us'" (§35). After all, "unless we recover the shared passion to create a community of belonging and solidarity worthy of our time, our energy and our resources, the global illusion that misled us will collapse and leave many in the grip of anguish and emptiness" (§36). The lack of a healthy global interconnectedness can also be observed in numerous other areas with far-reaching consequences; for example, in the domain of diverse human rights, given that "the right of some to free enterprise or market freedom cannot supersede the rights of peoples and the dignity of the poor, or, for that matter, respect for the natural environment" (§122). In addition, a potential (nuclear) war and armed conflicts of all kinds can "cause grave harm to societies, to the poor and vulnerable, to fraternal relations, to the environment and to cultural treasures, with irretrievable losses for the global community" (§257), showing how all this is not separated, but closely connected and inextricably intertwined.

The same idea of global interconnectedness is also addressed in FLOW as an important conceptual tool for understanding global inequalities and problems and for finding appropriate solutions in a concerted and integral way (§76–77). Consider, for instance, the following statement about an understanding of poverty in such a context and the intricate connection between environmental and social problems:

> In any nation, the poor are almost always the first to suffer as a result of any general adverse conditions, natural or social, economic or political. And, in many places, poverty is as much the result of racial or class discrimination as of mere personal misfortune. The current environmental crisis, for instance—anthropogenic climate change, toxic pollution of water sources and soils around the world, ubiquitous damage to the entire ecosystem by microplastics and other contaminants, deforestation, soil erosion, the rapid decline of biological diversity, and so forth—is an incalculable catastrophe for the entire planet and for all terrestrial life. Almost invariably, however, the greatest immediate burden falls upon the less economically developed quarters of the earth, where

governments can do—or elect to do—very little to protect the destitute against the consequences of industrial waste and general ecological devastation. It is the poor, moreover, who are most regularly displaced and further impoverished by the destruction of the environment around them. And, even in nations of the developed world, it tends to be the poorest citizens who are most routinely exposed to the dire results of environmental degradation and who lack the resources to remedy their situations. So long as immense discrepancies in wealth exist between nations and between individuals, social and political power will be the possession primarily of the rich, as will whatever degree of relative immunity from the consequences of human folly and corruption or natural calamity can be achieved by material means. So too will the best avenues of education or professional advancement, the best healthcare, the best legal protections, the best financial opportunities, the best access to institutions of political power, and so on. Great economic inequality is, inevitably, social injustice; it is, moreover, according to the teachings of Christ, a thing abominable in the eyes of God. (§41)

Second, another interesting point of convergence concerns the idea of a *universal fraternity* in all its articulations that especially permeate all of FT as its central theme. Here, this goes hand in hand with "acknowledging the dignity of each human person" so as to "contribute to the rebirth of a universal aspiration to fraternity.

Fraternity between all men and women" (§8). Or further:

> Social friendship and universal fraternity necessarily call for an acknowledgement of the worth of every human person, always and everywhere. If each individual is of such great worth, it must be stated clearly and firmly that "the mere fact that some people are born in places with fewer resources or less development does not justify the fact that they are living with less dignity." This is a basic principle of social life that tends to be ignored in a variety of ways by those who sense that it does not fit into their worldview or serve their purposes. (§106)

This key topic is also considered in the context of the innate tension between globalization and localization while avoiding both extremes:

> We need to have a global outlook to save ourselves from petty provincialism. When our house stops being a home and starts to become an enclosure, a cell, then the global comes to our rescue, like a "final cause" that draws us towards our fulfilment. At the same time, though, the local has to be eagerly embraced, for it possesses something that the global does not: it is capable of being a leaven, of bringing enrichment, of sparking mechanisms of subsidiarity. Universal fraternity and social friendship are thus two inseparable and equally vital poles in every society. To separate them would be to disfigure each and to create a dangerous polarization. (§142)

In fact, such ideas go so far as to propose a reform of the United Nations and other international economic institutions in the true sense of the ideal of "a family of nations" (§173), while the Church in its public role and responsibility may also contribute well to "the advancement of humanity and of universal fraternity" (§276). The existence of both Catholic and non-Catholic models for universal fraternity is underlined (§286), a fact that attests to the open and global agenda of the encyclical.

Interestingly enough, in FLOW the ideal of a universal fraternity is also repeatedly found and conceptualized within an Orthodox communitarian framework; for instance, with regard to slavery (§65), to the dialogue with the brothers and sisters of other faiths, Christian or otherwise (§50–60), or to migrants and generally displaced people (§67). Consider the following characteristic passage:

> To say we are made to serve God is to say we are made for loving communion: communion with the Kingdom of the Father and of the Son and of the Holy Spirit; and through communion with God as Trinity, human beings are also called into loving communion with their neighbors and the whole cosmos. Our actions are to flow from love of God and loving union with him in and through Christ, in whom we meet and treat our brother and sister as our very life. This communion with Christ in the face of our neighbor is what lies behind the

first and great commandment of the Law to love God with one's whole heart and one's neighbor as oneself (Matt 22:37–39). (§2)

Third, both documents try to articulate a *holistic and comprehensive view* of the current global situation and its multiple challenges. In this way, they move away from limited, incomplete, and fragmentary perceptions of the world that were typical of the perspective of (Western) modernity. Not accidentally, both documents reflect fundamental changes that have already taken place within the postmodern era, which has led to new views about humans and the world and about understanding the complex and multifaceted reality—holism being solely one particular case. In FT, this is most evident in the concept of "integral human development," which was already thematized in *Laudato Si'* as well. In this context, several significant deficits have been acknowledged: "Some economic rules have proved effective for growth, but not for integral human development. Wealth has increased, but together with inequality, with the result that 'new forms of poverty are emerging'" (§21). Or further: "Those who work for tranquil social coexistence should never forget that inequality and lack of integral human development make peace impossible" (§235). In fact, "seeking and pursuing the good of others and of the entire human family also implies helping individuals and societies to mature in the moral values that foster integral human development" (§112). There is no question that the Church shows a "constant attention to the common good and a concern for integral human development" (§276).

An analogous idea is also found in FLOW, which is also interested in enabling such a holistic human development and in transforming, improving, and renewing the overall condition of the world, understood as the environment and the peoples in connection. This is not surprising, since Orthodox theological thinking has always been characterized by holistic perspectives.[259] The understanding of the aforementioned interconnectedness of the entire world is, hence, crucial for such a holistic human development. Such an all-encompassing perspective is provided with a theological legitimation aimed at showing the unity of God's creation and the Church's mission in reminding humans of their responsibility in preserving it and contributing to cosmic harmony:

> None of us exists in isolation from the whole of humanity, or from the totality of creation. We are dependent creatures, creatures ever in communion, and hence we are also morally responsible not only for ourselves or for those whom we immediately influence or affect, but for the whole of the created order—the whole city of the cosmos, so to speak. In our own time, especially, we must understand that serving our neighbor and preserving the natural environment are

---

259 See Gillian Crow, "The Orthodox Vision of Wholeness," in Andrew Walker and Costa Carras, eds., *Living Orthodoxy in the Modern World: Orthodox Christianity and Society* (Crestwood, NY: St. Vladimir's Seminary Press, 2000), 7–22.

intimately and inseparably connected. There is a close and indissoluble bond between our care of creation and our service to the body of Christ, just as there is between the economic conditions of the poor and the ecological conditions of the planet. (§76)

We must also recall, moreover, that human beings are part of the intricate and delicate web of creation, and that their welfare cannot be isolated from the welfare of the whole natural world. As St. Maximus the Confessor argued, in Christ all the dimensions of humanity's alienation from its proper nature are overcome, including its alienation from the rest of the physical cosmos; and Christ came in part to restore to material creation its original nature as God's earthly paradise. Our reconciliation with God, therefore, must necessarily express itself also in our reconciliation with nature, including our reconciliation with animals. ... The unique grandeur of humanity in this world, the image of God within each person, is also a unique responsibility and ministry, a priesthood in service to the whole of creation in its anxious longing for God's glory. Humanity shares the earth with all other living things, but singularly among living creatures possesses the ability and authority to care for it (or, sadly, to destroy it). ... We must recall also that all the promises of scripture regarding the age that is to come concern not merely the spiritual destiny of humanity, but the future of a redeemed cosmos, in which plant and animal life are plentifully present, renewed in a condition of cosmic harmony. (§77)

As is to be expected, there are also differences between the two documents, which are not devoid of an appropriate explanation. As already mentioned, some of the theological presuppositions of both documents remain close to the respective traditions of these two Christian Churches. For instance, FLOW draws heavily on the biblical and Greek patristic tradition (e.g., Maximus the Confessor), while in FT the figure of Saint Francis of Assisi is dominant. Furthermore, as already stated, the Catholic document draws on the long and rich tradition of systematic reflection on social and philosophical questions, such as natural law. Such topics may be also traced in the Orthodox realm too,[260] yet reflection on them remains still rudimentary and unsystematic. Differences can also be observed as far as the addressees of the two documents are concerned. FLOW, on the one hand, is primarily written for and addressed to Orthodox Christians outlining a concomitant social ethos and responsibility (§82), although it also provides official information about Orthodoxy's positions on social issues to outside observers. FT, on the other hand, addresses not only Catholic believers, but

---

[260] See Guroian, "Notes," 234–236. See also Stanley S. Harakas, "The Natural Law Teaching of the Eastern Orthodox Church," *The Greek Orthodox Theological Review* 9 (1963–1964): 215–224; idem, "Eastern Orthodox Perspectives on Natural Law," *The American Journal of Jurisprudence* 24, no. 1 (1979): 86–113.

also all citizens of the world regardless of religion and culture, as well as institutions, governments, and societies dreaming of a better future; thus it intends to contribute to the idea of universal brotherhood. As Pope Francis noted: "Although I have written it from the Christian convictions that inspire and sustain me, I have sought to make this reflection an invitation to dialogue among all people of good will" (§6). The aforementioned explicit references to non-Catholics as models for imitation render the universal appeal of this document absolutely clear. After all, the Roman Catholic Church did not need to articulate a comprehensive social doctrine in the first place, unlike the Orthodox, thus the main focus of FT lies elsewhere. In addition, the overall method of argumentation in FT has been described as a rather inductive one, "where any reader is offered an interpretative key to reality," represented by the parable of the Good Samaritan, while in FLOW a more deductive process seems to predominate.[261]

More importantly, there are several differences regarding the degree of world affirmation in both documents. As already indicated, such an attitude is much more prevalent among the Western Churches (of course, to a varying degree) and still underscores their fundamental trajectories nowadays. It is worth mentioning that in FT Trinitarian, eucharistic (sacramental-liturgical), eschatological,

---

[261] See Samuele Bignotti, "Ecumenical Bridges between Orthodox and Catholic Sides: Comparison between *Fratelli Tutti* of Pope Francis and *For the Life of the World. Toward a Social Ethos of the Orthodox Church* Signed by the Ecumenical Patriarch Bartholomew," *Review of Ecumenical Studies – RES (Sibiu)* 13, no. 1 (2021): 42–50, at 45–46.

and similar perspectives, albeit presupposed, do not appear explicitly in the overall argumentation, which is strongly directed towards the affairs of this world. Basically, the same direction is also evident in the two prayers at the end of the encyclical, "A Prayer to the Creator" and "An Ecumenical Christian Prayer." On the contrary, the above elements appear to be prominent in FLOW and its overall argumentation. It is, thus, argued that "the social ethos of the Church is fulfilled not simply through the implementation of ethical prescriptions, but also and most fully in the liturgical expectation of the divine Kingdom" (§79). In fact, the Divine Liturgy is considered to be the main place where one learns a communal lifestyle and a concomitant ethos—always in close connection to the transcendental prototype, namely the heavenly liturgy (§5).

To avoid misunderstandings: All the above do not mean that Trinitarian, eucharistic, and eschatological elements are absent from or totally neglected in the Catholic social perspective. In fact, they are most explicitly present in the encyclical *Laudato Si'* (eucharistic in Section VI, §233–237; Trinitarian in Section VII, §238–240; and eschatological in Section IX, §243–245).[262] Simply, the main focus in FT lies elsewhere and attests to the stronger world affirmation on the Catholic side and to its intense socio-political concerns and commitments, which are not regarded as somehow secondary, but as instrumental, expressing hope for the realization of the Kingdom of God. Such a focus in this form is not usual on

---

262 See Lucas Briola, *The Eucharistic Vision of* Laudato Si': *Praise, Conversion, and Integral Ecology* (Washington, DC: Catholic University of America Press, 2023).

the Orthodox side, which always prefers to endow its world-related considerations with otherworldly dimensions that have decisively informed the Orthodox social presence and action across history. Social engagement is here primarily understood in connection with final salvation and redemption in eschatological terms. Not accidentally, the world is in FLOW repeatedly portrayed as fallen, broken, and corrupt (§4, 8, 18, 20, 22, 23, 29, 42, 45, 68, 73, 74) and needing to be transfigured in the light of God's Kingdom through Christian mission. Such a perspective is not lacking altogether from Catholic social documents, yet it is also complemented by a more constructive approach to this world from which numerous positive elements may still be drawn through responsible Christian action. This explains, for instance, why the development of a "political theology" has been very dominant in the Latin West generally over the last few centuries in contrast to the Orthodox East.[263] In other words, the redemptive message of the gospel acquires here a stronger grounding in this world through a necessary care for fellow human beings as neighbors, as indicated in the interpretation of the parable of the Good Samaritan in FT. It should be, however, emphasized that specific socio-historical events, developments, and circumstances led to this setting of priorities in East and West regarding their respective forms of world-relatedness. As a result,

---

263 See Vasilios N. Makrides, "Political Theology in Orthodox Christian Contexts: Specificities and Particularities in Comparison with Western Latin Christianity," in Kristina Stoeckl, Ingeborg Gabriel, and Aristotle Papanikolaou, eds., *Political Theologies in Orthodox Christianity: Common Challenges – Divergent Positions* (London: Bloomsbury T & T Clark, 2017), 25–54.

the above differences between them should neither be considered as normative, allegedly reflecting the "essence" of each Church respectively, nor as immutable entities beyond any change and necessary adaptation.

Another point of difference concerns the balance between the individual and the social elements in the two documents, as expressed in Catholic and Orthodox anthropology respectively. In the former case, the human being created in the image of God is characterized by both its individual and social dimensions, which are at the same time clearly distinct, yet always connected in the context of the relationship to oneself, to other human beings, and to society as a whole. In the latter case, this distinction is not accentuated as such, whereas the widespread idea of a communitarian lifestyle somehow blurs it.[264] After all, the strong anti-individualist tenor of various Orthodox discourses (especially over the last two centuries) and their wider impact should not be overlooked.[265] The same difference can also be observed in the distinction between individual/personal and social ethics (with

---

264 See Ursula Nothelle-Wildfeuer, "Gemeinsam unterwegs? Die neue orthodoxe Sozialethik und die katholische Soziallehre," *Religion & Gesellschaft in Ost und West (RGOW)* 48, no. 11 (November 2020): 26–28, at 26.

265 See Vasilios N. Makrides, "Gemeinschaftlichkeitsvorstellungen in Ost- und Südosteuropa und die Rolle der orthodox-christlichen Tradition," in Joachim von Puttkamer and Gabriella Schubert, eds., *Kulturelle Orientierungen und gesellschaftliche Ordnungsstrukturen in Südosteuropa* (Wiesbaden: Harrassowitz, 2010), 111–136; idem, "Orthodoxes Christentum und Individuum – verhängnisvolle Affäre oder produktive Interaktion?," in Bärbel Kracke, René Roux, and Jörg Rüpke, eds., *Die Religion des Individuums* (Münster: Aschendorff, 2013), 63–81, 188–190.

reference to justice in social orders, institutions, and structures), which is clear on the Catholic side, yet less so in FLOW.[266] All this has various repercussions for concrete topics; for instance, regarding the question of the inalienable dignity bestowed upon every human being by God that has led to the fundamental acceptance of human rights by both Catholics and Orthodox. Yet, the entire topic is reflected and pronounced upon more on the Catholic side as a means to a constructive dialogue with all people of good will, regardless of their specific provenance.[267]

Be that as it may, these points of divergence and their underlying theological and other principles do not matter much in the present comparison between the two documents and hardly render them incompatible. They simply reflect the historical, cultural, and theological particularities of each Church as well as its experience across time respectively. In other words, both documents can be considered as complementary without major difficulties. Both share a common concern for the world, the environment, social justice, human dignity, and solidarity among peoples and cultures worldwide. No doubt, there are lurking dangers in both Churches and cultures, which should not be ignored. On the one hand, the Western stronger world affirmation may lead to a concomitant greater worldliness of the Church in the sense of its worldly transformation, secularization, and oblivion of its eschatological dimension. On the other hand, the Orthodox otherworldliness

---

266 Nothelle-Wildfeuer, "Gemeinsam unterwegs?," 28
267 Nothelle-Wildfeuer, "Gemeinsam unterwegs?," 26–27.

may lead to a neglect of social issues and to the belief that social problems can only be finally solved eschatologically in an extra-historical framework. Both these excesses have been often observed in history, whereas a useful balance between these two trends would be certainly more than desirable. Most importantly, as both documents support the interconnectedness of all creation and the interdependence of all aspects of life, they appear to have taken into consideration the important changes effected within the current postmodern context. In fact, postmodernity has attempted to overcome the modern fragmentation of the world and all kinds of dualisms, Cartesian and otherwise, as well as to locate unexpected connections and interferences across the whole and rich spectrum of reality.[268]

Bearing all this in mind, both documents should be regarded as significant contributions to the ongoing conversation about the role of Christian Churches in shaping society and addressing social, political, environmental, and other issues in global terms. They both share a concern for promoting human dignity, social justice, and the common good and provide valuable insights and guidance for believers and non-believers alike. Hence, it is not accidental that the common Christian potential with regard to such issues

---

[268] See Johannes C. Wolfart, "Postmodernism," in Willi Braun and Russell T. McCutcheon, eds., *Guide to the Study of Religion* (London: Cassell, 2000), 380–395; Paul Heelas, "Postmodernism," in John R. Hinnells, ed., *The Routledge Companion to the Study of Religion* (Abington: Routledge, 2005), 259–274; Colin Campbell, "Modernity and Postmodernity," in Robert A. Segal, ed., *The Blackwell Companion to the Study of Religions* (Malden, MA: Blackwell, 2006), 309–320.

has given an incentive to look for a related Orthodox–Catholic rapprochement,[269] manifested by numerous common Catholic–Orthodox official statements[270] and other recent initiatives. For instance, there has been an international conference (Rome, March 31 – April 1, 2022) specifically on "Catholic and Orthodox Social Ethos after *Laudato Si'*: Christian Contributions to Civic Education in Europe," organized by the Catholic Central Institute for Social Sciences, together with the Konrad-Adenauer-Foundation, the Papal Dicastery for Promoting Integral Human Development, the Institute of Ecumenical Studies (University of Fribourg), and the scientific association "Ordo socialis."[271]

Speaking about a common responsibility for the world, Dietmar Schon has also tried to systematically chart the common ground between Orthodox and Catholics on a large variety of socio-ethical questions in the context of the current global age and its multiple challenges. Among other things, he compares each Church's theological principles that govern social ethics, such as the concept of humans in the image of God and the orientation towards the common good. He also examines various Orthodox–Catholic convergences in specific socio-ethical topics and subject

---

269 See Iuliu-Marius Morariu, "Ecology – Main Concern for the Christian Space of the 21st Century? Catholic and Orthodox Perspectives," *Journal for the Study of Religions and Ideologies* 19, no. 56 (Summer 2020): 124–135.

270 See Dietmar Schon, "Gemeinsame Erklärungen als Ausdruck schrittweiser Annäherung von Kirchen: Von Jerusalem bis nach Havanna und Lesbos," *Ostkirchliche Studien* 65 (2016): 201–238.

271 https://www.ksz.de/catholic-and-orthodox-social-ethos-after-laudato-si-christian-contributions-to-civic-education-in-europe/.

areas, such as the role of the Church in state and society, new accents for cooperation between Church and state, the Church as a socially relevant actor, personal life according to ethical values, ethical challenges in adolescence, interdenominational marriages, caring for the disabled, the sick, the elderly and the poor, end-of-life care and dealing with death and grief, material livelihoods and social justice, violence and war as ethical evils, the rejection of the doctrine of just war and the death penalty, ecumenical dialogue, readiness for inculturation, human rights and their fundamental importance, science, technology and the natural environment, as well as modern communication media and technologies[272]—to mention but a few. Critical points notwithstanding, he thus shows convincingly that there is impressive common ground between the two Churches that may well enable a common voice on a wide range of crucial and burning issues of today.

Concluding Remarks

The above comparative analysis of the two social documents, which have also attracted similar attention and comparative examination so far, has hopefully shown that both Churches are extremely interested in current social problems and issues and each tries to articulate their own vision and to provide answers out of their own Christian tradition and historical experience. Hence,

---

272 See Dietmar Schon, *Gemeinsame Verantwortung für die Welt? Orthodox-katholische Annäherung in sozialethischen Fragen* (Regensburg: Friedrich Pustet, 2023).

it is not surprising that both documents aim at integral human development and an improvement of the overall condition in the world, including both the natural environment and the peoples who inhabit it (e.g., through justice, mercy, social commitment, civil society, and integral ecology). The differences in perspectives and accentuations that may still be discerned are more or less expected and do not really separate the two Churches, which seem to be ready to learn and profit from each other in various domains. For example, the Orthodox side has still to address the issue of modernity in a more systematic and thorough way by critically drawing on the experience of Western Churches (especially of Roman Catholicism[273]) and by remodeling its own identity accordingly. FLOW is already a testament to important steps in this direction, yet it is still a process that needs perseverance, continuity, and determination in order to bear fruit in the long run. Given that various Orthodox Churches (e.g., the Russian one) and various Orthodox rigorist circles react against this Orthodox *aggiornamento*,[274] the way towards this end is quite complicated and thorny.

Aside from numerous other examples, the fruitful exchange between the two Churches is already clearly evident in the

---

273   See Vasilios N. Makrides, "Der konstruktive Umgang mit der Moderne – oder was die Orthodoxie vom Katholizismus zu lernen vermag," in Dietmar Schon, ed., *Identität und Authentizität von Kirchen im "globalen Dorf": Annäherung von Ost und West durch gemeinsame Ziele?* (Regensburg: Friedrich Pustet, 2019), 103–127.

274   See Vasilios N. Makrides, "Orthodox Christian Rigorism: Attempting to Delineate a Multifaceted Phenomenon," *Interdisciplinary Journal for Religion and Transformation in Contemporary Society* 2, no. 2 (July 2016): 216–252.

documents under discussion. In FT, Pope Francis stated clearly that "in the preparation of *Laudato Si'*, I had a source of inspiration in my brother Bartholomew, the Orthodox Patriarch, who has spoken forcefully of our need to care for creation" (§5). More extensive references to the positions and actions of Ecumenical Patriarch Bartholomew regarding ecology and environmental problems as well as their spiritual and ethical roots are found in *Laudato Si'* (§7–9). All this can be interpreted as a positive sign towards a continuing dialogue, mutual understanding, and cooperation not only in social issues, but also in many other domains. No doubt, the long historical interactions between the two Churches have been marked in many respects by conflict, opposition, and even hatred—to a large extent, for understandable reasons, due to the final schism and the centuries-old deep estrangement between them. Nevertheless, this should not obfuscate the fact that productive and creative encounters between them were not out of the ordinary, even in times of tension.[275] Anti-Catholic positions linger on even today among the Orthodox, often within an overall anti-Western and anti-ecumenical framework.[276] Some related controversial

---

275 See Katrin Boeckh and Dietmar Schon, eds., *Der Blick auf den Anderen: Katholisch-Orthodoxe Selbst- und Fremdwahrnehmung* (Regensburg: Friedrich Pustet, 2021); Ioan Moga, *Orthodoxe Selbst- und Fremdbilder: Identitätsdiskurse der rumänischen orthodoxen Theologie des 20. Jh. im Verhältnis zur Römisch-Katholischen Kirche* (Göttingen: Vandenhoeck & Ruprecht, 2020).

276 See Vasilios N. Makrides, "Orthodoxer Antiokzidentalismus und Antikatholizismus. Aktuelle Entwicklungen und Anpassungsprozesse," in Dietmar Schon, ed., *Dialog 2.0 – Braucht der orthodox-katholische Dialog neue Impulse?* (Regensburg: Friedrich Pustet, 2017), 134–159.

discussions during the pan-Orthodox Council of Crete attest to this.[277] Conservative Orthodox and Catholics, often in collaboration with others, still try to create transreligious alliances in order to oppose modernity and globalization.[278] At the same time, things have certainly changed over the last decades, as there are also clear signs of a serious rapprochement, mutual understanding, and collaboration in specific domains between the two Churches. In this context, it is also encouraging to observe that Catholics have also engaged in recent years more systematically in finding points of convergence with the Orthodox on various pressing global issues.[279] From this perspective, social documents such FLOW and FT should be evaluated as corresponding and complementary, testifying to the common Christian heritage and responsibility for the global world and the natural environment. Needless to say, the "Halki Summit" series of workshops[280] and other related initiatives

---

277 See Theresia Hainthaler, "Nach der 'Heiligen und Großen Synode' von Kreta 2016: Fragen und Überlegungen zu einem Neuansatz des orthodox-katholischen Dialogs," in Dietmar Schon, ed., *Dialog 2.0 – Braucht der orthodox-katholische Dialog neue Impulse?* (Regensburg: Friedrich Pustet, 2017), 118–133; Alexandru-Marius Crişan, "The Council of Crete and its Perception of Other Churches," in Katrin Boeckh and Dietmar Schon, eds., *Der Blick auf den Anderen: Katholisch-Orthodoxe Selbst- und Fremdwahrnehmung* (Regensburg: Friedrich Pustet, 2021), 192–222.

278 See Daniel P. Payne and Jennifer M. Kent, "An Alliance of the Sacred: Prospects for a Catholic-Orthodox Partnership Against Secularism in Europe," *Journal of Ecumenical Studies* 46, no. 1 (2011): 41–66.

279 See Dietmar Schon, ed., *Dialog 2.0 – Braucht der orthodox-katholische Dialog neue Impulse?* (Regensburg: Friedrich Pustet, 2017).

280 https://www.halkisummit.com/.

are clearly part of this influential and successful global agenda that brings people together from across many countries, religions, and cultures including Catholics and Orthodox; thus it should be supported and continued at any price.

10. ENVIRONMENTAL CRISIS, ANTHROPOLOGICAL CRISIS: AT THE ROOT OF THE ECOLOGICAL CRISIS

Sergio Rondinara

For this brief reflection on the environmental crisis I take my cue from the third chapter of Pope Francis' encyclical letter *Laudato Si'*. This encyclical letter on the care of our common home has the merit of taking up central instances of the social doctrine of the Catholic Church in tune with certain features of the contemporary mindset, to the point of being a true work of inculturation of the gospel.

In §101 we read: "It would hardly be helpful to describe symptoms without acknowledging the human origins of the ecological crisis. A certain way of understanding human life and activity has gone awry, to the serious detriment of the world around us." In few words, this statement highlights and underlines the anthropological nature and relevance of the environmental crisis.

I would like to draw your attention to this very point. If in the past the relationship between the human person and nature was a balanced and often collaborative one—just think of the agricultural and rural society—today it has taken on a critical configuration which we refer to as the *environmental crisis*. With this expression, we bitterly express the deterioration of the relationship between human society and the natural environment, that is typical of industrialized countries, but which is now spreading to every latitude. On the other hand, the anthropological character of such a crisis—in its both individual and social aspects—can be felt immediately insofar as human action is both the cause and the place—the means—for its solution. In fact, recognizing and taking responsibility for a problem we have generated is the first and necessary step towards its solution.

The environmental crisis refers to a crisis that is broader and deeper than what we observe; it invests the human person in his or her entirety, it is an *anthropological crisis*. On the other hand, this environmental crisis refers to a deeper crisis that affects the human person as a whole. It is the alarm bell of a profound anthropological crisis, the daughter of a specific conception that the modern and contemporary person has of themselves. A person, and therefore a humanity, who, in the search for their own self-realization, conformed more to *homo faber* than to *homo sapiens*, and made themselves the absolute master of their own destiny and nature.

Again in chapter three, the encyclical's analysis rightly proposes to focus attention both on what is called the dominant *technocratic paradigm*, i.e., on that model of development marked by the dominance of technology and its rationality over the actions of the human person with respect to the natural world, and on the rather mechanistic view of the natural world as inert, without quality and easily assimilated into a storehouse of resources, a view implicitly endorsed by modern and contemporary economics.

However, in addition to these points highlighted by the encyclical, there are other moments that we can grasp of the anthropological character of the environmental crisis. The first, of a general nature, can be identified through the environmental unsustainability of the current development model. Already at the beginning of this millennium, the average ecological footprint[281] of humanity as a whole was estimated to be one third greater than the available surface area on our planet. In other words, more than 20 years ago, humanity's consumption was already one-third greater than what the earth's natural system was capable of continuously regenerating each year.

We are consuming, or rather, we are eroding the natural capital of our earth's system, without taking any account of the opportunities that, by our actions, we are denying to future generations that in time will replace us on the planet. This is an intergenerational ethical duty that we should keep in mind because it is a duty

---

281   The ecological footprint is an indicator that estimates the impact of our being and living on the natural environment of the Earth's system. Cf. Mathis Wackernagel and William Rees, *Our Ecological Footprint: Reducing Human Impact on the Earth* (Philadelphia: New Society Publishers, 1996); translated into Italian as *L'impronta ecologica: Come ridurre l'impatto dell'uomo sulla terra* (Milan: Edizioni Ambiente, 2004).

recognized by our moral conscience. We can easily identify the current environmental crisis with our extraordinary capacity to harvest, circulate, and consume energy and raw materials (a significant part of which are non-renewable) insofar as the current technological system can allow industrial groups or individuals to move such a quantity of material and energy resources that they alter the planet's environmental balance.

A second aspect that shows us how the environmental crisis is an anthropological crisis can be seen in the *social injustice* that accompanies resource management on a global level. Nowadays, the world's population uses incredibly different portions of natural capital to sustain themselves, depending on where they live. This allows us to address the environmental crisis as an unbalanced distribution of natural resources. In this respect, the category of justice inevitably comes into play. In fact, according to assessments obtained through the above-mentioned ecological footprint methodology, we can group the various countries of the planet into three categories:

1) countries rich in both environmental and financial resources. These mostly manage to balance their ecological footprint;
2) countries rich mainly in financial resources but which, due to their lifestyle or natural deficiencies, have a high biological deficit;

3) finally, countries rich in the environment but not in financial resources. These countries balance or even have a biological capacity that exceeds their per capita consumption.

Looking at this picture, if we ask ourselves where and how countries with an ecological deficit get the natural resources they consume, the answer is immediate: these resources come into their possession through importation. In this case, it is precisely the social and environmental impact of the world trade in raw materials that needs to be scrutinized under the category of justice. Some study groups and international bodies believe that the current way in which goods, including environmental goods, are bought and sold is quite unfair, as free trade, without customs barriers, between countries with disproportionately different financial capacities, can only generate inequalities. Because of these mechanisms, a World Environment Organization (WTE) is being called for from many sides,[282] to operate alongside the World Trade Organization (WTO), and to have the task of making the rules of free trade and environmental protection compatible with each other, as well as enforcing them on all parties. In the current situation, those with financial power can easily access natural goods in countries with weak economies, and they pay lucrative prices for their profit margins. This is a well-known trend that is known as environmental

---

[282] Cf. Amedeo Postiglione, "Il governo mondiale dell'ambiente," in Amedeo Postiglione and Antonio Pavan, eds., *Etica, ambiente, sviluppo* (Rome: Edizioni Scientifiche Italiane, 2001), 201–241; Stefano Zamagni, "Dopo il WTO è necessario il WEO," *Etica per le professioni* 5 (2003–2003): 17–24.

dumping, i.e., the selling off of natural goods by a country because it lacks measures to protect them or to regulate their extraction. Alongside it emerges a second phenomenon called social dumping, where natural goods are cheap because the workers involved in their extraction and initial processing receive very low wages and almost always lack union and social security insurance cover.

A third anthropological aspect can be identified in the decline in the *quality of life*. The term "quality of life" refers to both being healthy and feeling well and is defined by physical and psychological attributes. If we were to investigate the environmental crisis from the aspect of human health, we would find that it is identified with the emergence of new diseases and the growing spread of some already known. Moreover, while we tend to live in increasingly artificial environments, within ourselves we are increasingly seeking an approach to and enjoyment of nature that is non-invasive and respectful of its harmonies. Deep down we are seeking a pristine, untouched nature, so that we can acknowledge and contemplate an otherness—other than ourselves—that we yearn for.

In addition to those just mentioned, I would like to highlight an additional aspect of the environmental crisis. Understood as an anthropological crisis, it appears before our eyes as a semantic crisis, a crisis of meaning. We are increasingly losing our ability to recognize and give lasting meanings and consequently the values of nature. We are also increasingly losing our ability to give lasting meanings to natural objects, meanings that are not dictated by utilitarian logic or mere commercial value.

Personally, I believe, and here is the thesis of this reflection, that a renewed person–nature relationship, appropriate for today, necessarily passes through the recovery—or in some cases through a new acquisition—of the meanings of the relationships that bind each of us to our natural habitat and to all of nature, on earth and otherwise. But how is it possible to recover the meaning of the relationships that bind us to nature? This question is a significant cultural challenge since we need to undertake wide-ranging research that shows us the semantic richness of the terms "person," "nature," and the "relationships" that exist between them.

Such a challenge, because of its inherent cultural scope, can only be structured on multiple levels of human action. These include the cultural anthropological level, the level of thought, the ethical level, and the religious level. These various levels constitute many paths for the recovery of the meanings we are seeking and at the same time are also like many moments of a personal and social *educational path* to be explored. With such a vast research, in this essay I will only focus on the religious level, referring only to the Christian moment.

The question of how we can gain new meanings or recover lost meanings of the relationships that bind us to nature is a challenge for people of faith. In the search for an adequate and renewed relationship with nature, they are called upon to also make the component of the revealed message that concerns our relationship with the natural world, become part of culture. Today, as never before, the environmental issue presents itself as a privileged locus where faith is directly challenged and where we are invited to give the reasons for our hope, as the First Letter of Peter reminds us (1 Pet 3:15).

In the current context, Christian faith is called upon, not so much for an apologetic response to those who have accused Christianity[283] of being the main cause of the current ecological crisis, but rather because, for the believer, the full semantic recovery of the relationship between person and nature implies the rediscovery of one's relationship with nature in the light of the entire relationship presented by Revelation. Such an itinerary can be undertaken according to the threefold perspective of time: past, present, and future; which in the horizon of Revelation becomes: protological past, historical present, and eschatological future.

---

283 Cf. Lynn Townsend White, Jr., "The Historical Roots of Our Ecologic Crisis," *Science* 155, no. 3767 (March 10, 1967): 1203–1207; Italian translation, "Le radici storico-culturali della nostra crisi ecologica," *Il Mulino* 226 (1973): 251–263; Carl Amery, *Das Ende der Vorsehung: Die gnadenlosen Folgen des Christentums* (Reinbek: Rowohlt, 1972); Eugen Drewermann, "Der tödliche Fortschritt: Von der Zerstörung der Erde und des Menschen," in *Erbe des Christentums* (Regensburg: Ed. Pustet, 1981); Umberto Galimberti, *Psiche e techne: L'uomo nell'età della tecnica* (Milan: Feltrinelli, Milano), 293–295. For more information, cf. "Les accusateurs," in Cédric de La Serre, *Les chrétiens sont-ils responsables de la crise écologique?* (Paris: Salvator, 2020), 21–35.

In the light of this threefold perspective, the terms "human person" and "nature" can be re-semantized, and consequently revalued. Indeed, in the light of faith:

1) *nature* can be fully valued because it is recognized that as creation, it has an intrinsic value, a value in itself, independent of that attributed to it by humanity in its economic or utilitarian calculations; moreover it is recognized that in nature there is a manifestation of God that is a gift of Himself (Rom 1:20) and its ultimate purpose is known: to be the physical foundation for the new heavens and new earth prophesied by Isaiah and announced in Revelation (cf. Isa 66:22; Rom 8:22; 2 Pet 3:13; Rev 21:1).

2) the *network of relationships* that binds it to us can be enhanced as we become aware that we are fellow travellers towards the final recapitulation (Eph 1:3–10) where God will be all in all things (1 Cor 15:24–28).

3) lastly, the creative role that the *human person* has in leading nature to God can be valued since he/she understands him/herself as a mediator, as a priest of nature,[284] capable of improving it and guiding it towards a fullness that we do not yet possess and involving it in the cultural development of humanity through human work.

---

284 Cf. John Zizioulas, *Il creato come eucaristia* (Magnano: Edizioni Qiqajon, 1994), 47ff.

At this point, however, Christian thought is called upon to take a step forward. In the light of this threefold valorization and corresponding semanticization, it is called upon to clearly reconfigure its own anthropocentric position derived from the Genesis texts (cf. Gen 1, in particular Gen 1:27–28; 2:15). Such an undertaking would have a great cultural impact, especially in the ethical field where today the countless doctrines on environmental ethics are characterized essentially by fundamental approaches that are totally at odds with each other.

In this context, the *anthropocentric* position, strongly marked by economic liberalism, tends to affirm the fundamental difference between humanity and all the natural elements that constitute its habitat. The basis of this position is the assumption that the human person has a vital role within the natural world and the latter does not possess its own intrinsic value, but rather has only the value that the person gives it.

The second approach, the physio-centric one, marked by environmental thinking, affirms the preservation of nature regardless of human interests. The latter, belonging to nature like any other biotic element, must live in harmony with it, complying with its laws.

Now, as mentioned above, Christian thought is invited to redefine the character of anthropocentrism in the texts of Genesis.

Which is the equivalent of asking: "What is the anthropocentrism for a rising environmental ethic in the Christian context?" The answer can only be found in the view of the "Christ event," the heart of Christian anthropology. This event will mark the characteristic of Christian ethics regarding natural reality. The "Christ event" brings about a radical transformation of the human person, for as the Apostle Paul states in Second Corinthians, "If anyone is in Christ, the new creation has come: The old has gone, the new is here!" (2 Cor 5:17). They are therefore a *new creature*, not only because redeemed from the situation of non-love where sin relegated them, but because *the very agape* of the Father (that is, the very Love with which the Father loves the Son) has been poured into their heart and which now dwells in them (cf. Rom 5:5), and fills them with the Spirit of God Himself.

In Jesus we have truly become *children in the Son*, we participate in the very Life of God, to the point that the Holy Spirit dwells in us, crying out "Abba, Father" (cf. Rom 8:15; Gal 4:6). When we are enfolded in Jesus and filled with His Love, we discover that we are bound together by a deep bond of unity, that we are "one" with each other in that we are "one in Christ Jesus" (Gal 3:28), as the Letter to the Galatians tells us. We are no longer individuals reduced to the narrow dimensions of our existence, but open to the "I" of Jesus, we are also open to all men and women, we are, as Cyril of Jerusalem affirmed,[285] *consanguineous* and *concorporeal* with Jesus and with each other.

We thus become the leaven of unity for all creation (human and otherwise); we become people who:

- compose in unity not only their own inner dimension and the various expressions of human life (sociality, politics, science, economics) but also peoples and cultures.
- prepare by their action, through their own work, the fulfilment of the cosmos (cf. Rom 8:19–21).

This is the type of human person, a new creature, who defines the type of anthropocentrism of Christian ethics, a Christian *anthropocentrism, an oblative anthropocentrism* whose ontological weight, with great difficulty, manages to exist within the phenomenal classifications of current philosophical or sociological analyses. Thus, the human person is at the center of the relationship with nature. In realizing the gift of self, they become more and more themselves insofar as they live as children of God, and live in full reciprocity with their fellow human beings to the point of being "one heart and one mind" (Acts 4:32) with them. And they draw humanity and the natural world towards the very Life of God. In *oblative anthropocentrism* the unique traits of the human person, such as creativity and technical ability, are safeguarded without him/her degenerating into a hypertrophic self-understanding of his or her "self" and abilities. Moreover, this form of anthropocentrism

---

285 Cyril of Jerusalem, *Cat. Myst* 4.3; PG 33.1100.

conveys and nurtures in each person and in society a culture of self-giving. Finally, nature is also preserved because of the recovery of all the meanings it takes on in light of the threefold appreciation.

This is nothing more than the realization of the triple vocation that according to Genesis has distinguished human beings ever since God created them:

- created them in His image and likeness (called to communion with God),
- created them in the reciprocity of man/woman (called to communion with other human beings), and
- created them and entrusted them with the earth (called to communion with the cosmos).

But all this needs to be brought into the present, to be reversed in the history of our times, and this requires an ecological conversion, as the prophetic teachings of Patriarch Bartholomew[286] and Pope Francis[287] remind us.

Conclusion

The challenge posed by the environmental crisis demands and calls for an anthropological model (a certain kind of man and woman, a type of person)—for the most part still unheard of today—in which the human person is understood neither as a dominator

---

286 Ecumenical Patriarch Bartholomew, *Il patto di Patmos*, in *Grazia cosmica, umile preghiera: La visione ecologica del patriarca ecumenico di Costantinopoli Bartolomeo I*, ed. John Chryssavgis (Florence: Libreria Editrice Fiorentina, 2007).
287 LS, §217.

according to the anthropocentric perspective, nor as a common biotic element according to the physio-centric perspective, but as a conscious and responsible subject who is part of nature but who in his/her transcendence realizes himself/herself existentially in his/her giving of themselves, that is, in implementing the gift of self to his/her fellow men and women, and to the natural reality of which she/he is also part. Hence an anthropological model in which we move from a predominantly individual perspective to a communal perspective, from a limited group perspective to a global human family perspective. And here every authentic religious and cultural tradition is called upon to give its contribution.

V. CONCLUSION

11. ADDRESSING THE ECOLOGICAL CRISIS TOGETHER: ECUMENICAL PERSPECTIVES IN ECO-THEOLOGY

Metropolitan Job of Pisidia

The Orthodox Church has been a pioneer in addressing the environmental crisis since 1986. This led the Ecumenical Patriarchate to take an active part in various international ecological initiatives and to establish September 1 as a day of prayer for the protection of the natural environment in 1989. In the very first Patriarchal Encyclical issued in 1989, the late Ecumenical Patriarch Demetrios of blessed memory asserted that the Church could not remain indifferent before the ecological crisis and called "all those entrusted with the responsibility of governing the nations to act without delay taking all necessary measures for the protection and preservation of the natural creation."

The Ecumenical Patriarchate has chosen the beginning of the new liturgical year (September 1) as the "Day of Protection for the Environment," when prayers of thanksgiving are offered to the

Creator for "the great gift of creation" as well as supplications for its preservation. Given its coincidence with the time of harvest, it is also appropriate to realize how much we owe to our Creator, in the same spirit as the feast of Thanksgiving observed in North America during the fall.

This initiative of the Ecumenical Patriarchate was very well received in the ecumenical movement, by the WCC and the CEC, as well as by different Christian churches such as the Roman Catholic Church, the Anglican communion, the Lutheran World Federation, and the World Communion of Reformed Churches.

No other worldwide religious leader has placed the ecological crisis at the forefront of his service and sermons as has our Ecumenical Patriarch Bartholomew. We are glad that his clear message was heard and taken up by other religious leaders, including Pope Francis. The papal encyclical *Laudato Si'*, Pope Francis' second encyclical, which was officially published in June 2015, has led to many Roman Catholic initiatives for lifestyle changes that reflect respect for creation, "our common home." In three paragraphs of his encyclical (nos. 7–9), Pope Francis gives credit to Ecumenical Patriarch Bartholomew for his contribution on this crucial matter. "Patriarch Bartholomew has spoken in particular of the need for each of us to repent of the ways we have harmed the planet," writes the Pope. "He has repeatedly stated this firmly and persuasively, challenging us to acknowledge our sins against creation." He further adds:

> At the same time, Bartholomew has drawn attention to the ethical and spiritual roots of environmental problems, which require that we look for solutions not only in technology but in a change of humanity; otherwise we would be dealing merely with symptoms. He asks us to replace consumption with sacrifice, greed with generosity, wastefulness with a spirit of sharing, an asceticism which "entails learning to give, and not simply to give up."[288]

In the same spirit, the environmental crisis was also discussed by the Holy and Great Council of the Orthodox Church gathered on Crete in 2016. Its message emphasized the spiritual and moral causes of the ecological crisis connected with greed, avarice, and egoism, which lead to over-exploitation of natural resources, pollution, and climate change. For this reason, it stated that "the Christian response to the problem demands repentance for the abuses, an ascetic frame of mind as an antidote to overconsumption, and at the same time a cultivation of the consciousness that man is a steward and not a possessor of creation."[289]

The Council saw the origin of the problem in a secular approach to the environment which introduces a rupture between creation

---

288 *Laudato Si'*, §8–9.
289 Holy and Great Council, *Message*, §8. Cf. also *The Mission of the Orthodox Church in Today's World*, §F.10.

and the Creator. For this reason, as the encyclical of the Council reminds us,

> The approach to the ecological problem on the basis of the principles of the Christian tradition demands not only repentance for the sin of the exploitation of the natural resources of the planet, namely, a radical change in mentality and behavior, but also asceticism as an antidote to consumerism, the deification of needs and the acquisitive attitude. It also presupposes our greatest responsibility to hand down a viable natural environment to future generations and to use it according to divine will and blessing.[290]

Following the papal encyclical *Laudato Si'*, which was the first papal encyclical to address the theme of the protection of creation, and following the Holy and Great Council of the Orthodox Church, Pope Francis and Ecumenical Patriarch Bartholomew issued a joint message for the World Day of Prayer for Creation on September 1, 2017. This message invited all people of good will to dedicate a time of prayer for the environment on September 1, stressed that "the human environment and the natural environment are deteriorating together, and this deterioration of the planet weighs upon the most vulnerable of its people," and proclaimed that "the urgent call and

---

[290] Holy and Great Council, *Encyclical*, §V.14.

challenge to care for creation are an invitation for all of humanity to work towards sustainable and integral development."[291]

In the same spirit, the Lutheran World Federation, at its Twelfth Assembly in Windhoek in 2017, clearly pointed out that salvation, humans, and creation are not for sale and urged the development of alternative economic models that could be practiced on large and small scales. The Twenty-Sixth General Council of the World Communion of Reformed Churches in Leipzig in 2017 called for churches to present themselves as beacons of change and alternative communities amidst growing socio-economic and ecological challenges.

Since its Tenth Assembly in Busan (Korea) in 2013, the World Council of Churches has called for a pilgrimage towards an "Economy of Life" and climate justice. The ecological crisis, seen through the lens of protection of God's creation, has since been at the center of attention in the different programs of the WCC.

Having undertaken measures to improve children's well-being in response to a request received at the 2013 Assembly in Busan, the WCC developed a special program called "Churches' Commitments to Children," which is an open invitation and living resource for the ecumenical commitment to child well-being, uniting the churches for children in their pilgrimage of justice and peace. This program

---

[291] Ecumenical Patriarch Bartholomew and Pope Francis, Joint Message on the World Day of Creation, September 1, 2017. http://w2.vatican.va/content/francesco/en/messages/pont-messages/2017/documents/papa-francesco_20170901_messaggio-giornata-cura-creato.html.

supports engagement of churches in three specific areas: child protection, child participation, and climate justice initiatives with children. Concerning the last area, it supports initiatives to educate and to involve children and adolescents regarding environmental issues and particularly the question of climate change. The development and implementation of this program is supported by the United Nations Children's Fund (UNICEF) through a global WCC-UNICEF partnership, with a focus on ending violence against children and climate justice.

The Ecumenical Patriarchate replied positively to this program, and Patriarch Bartholomew personally addressed the World Children's Day Celebratory Event in Geneva in November 2018, where he stated the following:

> Children are especially vulnerable to climate change and environmental degradation. When water becomes scarce because of drought, the poorest children and families are most likely to resort to unsafe water sources. ... Any abuse of our earth's resources—and, above all, of water as the source and symbol of life and renewal—contradicts our sacred and social obligation to other people, and especially to those who live in poverty and in the margins of society. Water is a fundamental good, which must be accessible for all people

regardless of race, gender, ethnicity, socioeconomic status or any other aspect of discrimination.[292]

On that occasion, the Ecumenical Patriarch stressed that the issues of immigration, refugees, and climate change are closely linked and will remain the biggest global challenges that our world will have to face in the coming years. He mentioned climate change as a primary cause of child immigration and considered that it represents a serious threat to their lives. Therefore, according to him, the protection of children is closely linked with the protection of the environment, toward which our churches must undertake appropriate initiatives.

The most recent World Council of Churches resource oriented toward the congregational level of churches' engagement in ecological and economic justice is a document entitled "Roadmap for Congregations, Communities, and Churches for an Economy of Life and Ecological Justice."[293] It is a very practical invitation to our parishes to join a pilgrimage for an Economy of Life and climate justice, to commit to make changes in the way people live, to share successful ideas, and to encourage one another. It offers a five-step program to change the way we deal with the economy and our ecological surroundings in the following areas: living in accordance

---

292   https://www.oikoumene.org/en/resources/documents/other-meetings/keynote-address-by-his-all-holiness-ecumenical-patriarch-bartholomew-at-the-world-childrens-day.

293   https://www.oikoumene.org/en/resources/documents/wcc-programmes/diakonia/economy-of-life/roadmap-for-congregations-communities-and-churches-for-an-economy-of-life-and-ecological-justice.

with the covenant with God and creation, renewable energy and climate protection, just and sustainable consumption, economies of life, and networking.

By living in accordance with the covenant with God and creation, the document calls Christian communities to support and practice small-scale, life-giving agriculture, create community gardens, and provide access to clean water. As we all believe, food and water are a gift from God and therefore are a human right. Unfortunately, the conventional industrial agriculture is leading to a critical loss of biodiversity, disastrous effects of climate change, degradation of the soil that nourishes us, and sometimes to land grabs and displacement of people by greedy multinational companies. The document invites our parishes to contribute to resolve this problem by organizing community gardens that yield vegetables, medicinal herbs, fruits, or rare species which can rescue biodiversity. Gardening could be a fun activity for our Sunday schools as well as for our older parishioners. Such gardens can be wonderful meeting points and help to deepen relationships within the community. They are also visible examples of practicing life-giving agriculture and rediscovering all resources for food sovereignty in accordance with God's creation. Parishes should also respect the human right to water, promote water as a public good, and say no to bottled water where tap water is safe, or look for alternatives where it is not.

By promoting renewable energy and climate protection, the document calls us to monitor energy consumption and move towards renewable energies, promote climate-friendly mobility, and deal with energy and materials consciously. It invites our parishes based in privileged countries to control the use of energy and to improve the energy efficiency of buildings and establishments. Where possible, changing from conventional to eco-electricity is the first and easiest step, by installing, for instance, solar panels, building a community-run, small-scale hydroelectric dam, etc. Also, posting timetables for public transport, bicycle parking and sharing, setting up one of the many carpooling or car-sharing systems, installing charging points for electric cars, or, above all, reducing the need for mobility by re-regionalizing the daily life economy, are practical projects which are suggested to be undertaken by parishes. The faithful of our churches have to be reminded that the production of an item requires energy and that every waste of energy harms the environment and costs money that could be used for beneficial projects.

As our Ecumenical Patriarch pointed out during his memorable visit to the WCC headquarters on April 24, 2017, "Ecologists today are giving us a wake-up call, saying that by 2050, the oceans will contain more plastic than fish by weight. Plastic pollution is an environmental and social justice issue. This is why we should be avoiding plastic by using alternatives in our everyday life."[294] This alarming call should not remain only pious words but should be taken into concrete action by our parishioners. Parishes can implement small changes like duplex printing on recycled paper,

---

294 https://www.oikoumene.org/en/resources/documents/other-meetings/address-of-his-all-holiness-ecumenical-patriarch-bartholomew.

avoiding plastic and styrofoam cups, or installing switchable electrical outlets, which can have a remarkable effect.

The document calls for a just and sustainable consumption by buying ecological, fair, and regional, reducing waste, and recycling. Supporting local establishments promotes economic well-being and coherence in our regions and has a positive impact on the environment. For this reason, it invites our parishes to officially introduce the "best offer" principle, as opposed to the "cheapest offer." For instance, meals in our parishes can provide fairly traded coffee, tea, juice, and chocolate, and vegetarian food. Promoting vegetarian food is something the Orthodox, who have such a strong tradition of fasting, could easily do in periods of fasting, during which the environmental dimension should be underlined, taking into consideration experiences such as "fasting for climate justice" that was taken up by the World Lutheran Federation.[295] They should purchase products that adhere to social and ecological standards, and long-lasting products. The huge and still growing plastic island in the ocean is showing how we drown in our own rubbish. Plastic is even becoming a part of our food chain. The document reminds us that there is no need to use beverages in plastic bottles and calls us to reduce waste and encourage recycling.

The document speaks also of economies of life, inviting communities to create places for moneyless interaction, and to practice alternative economic models and just finance. It suggests

---

295   https://www.lutheranworld.org/sites/default/files/Fasting%20for%20 Climate%20Justice_A%20Lutheran%20Perspective.pdf.

that in a world where daily life is more and more dominated by consumerism, and achievements are increasingly measured in terms of money, our parishes can become a meeting point without the necessity of buying or paying for anything, without judgment of ability to pay, without exclusion. The document suggests a very simple beginning: a shelf where people can deposit things they no longer need and others can take items for free, organizing free shops, second-hand shops, food-sharing-points, repair cafés, skills-exchange networks, producer–consumer networks, and much more. It points out that churches often critique the destructive economy and at the same time empower it by thoughtless investment. It underlines that there are many good methods we can use in favor of our communities and the world.

Finally, the document emphases networking. It suggests naming contact persons for economic and ecological justice, to raise our voice on economic and ecological issues in our communities and beyond and to network with other communities and initiatives. It suggests that when a parish names contact persons, they feel encouraged in what they do. Exchange with others brings new ideas and higher motivation. Such a project should have an ecumenical dimension. Our parishes should be networking with other neighboring Christian communities. Regional projects can more easily be realized if local promoters are clearly identified. It is encouraging and joyful to be part of a movement, to build alliances with other congregations, communities, and initiatives in our own countries and worldwide. We need to look for good initiatives in our surroundings, and to learn from, accompany, and share them.

With such practical ideas, one can see how Orthodox "eco-theology" has impacted the ecumenical circles! As thirty years have passed since the Ecumenical Patriarchate declared in a prophetic way the feast of September 1 as the day of prayer for the protection of creation, inviting people of good will around the world to pray and to undertake proper and responsible actions to preserve it, many things have been said, very little has been done. This critique ought to be addressed to every one of us, including us the Orthodox.

The time has come for us to implement our ortho-doxy by an ecological ortho-praxis, or in other words to incarnate our eco-theology by an eco-justice in each one of our parishes.

Discontinuing the use of plastic bottles and utensils, reducing waste, encouraging recycling, planting trees, organizing community gardens, promoting vegetarian food, promoting climate-friendly mobility, installing solar panels are very simple things that we can do at the level of our parishes, thus witnessing and teaching people what they ought to do in their homes. I remember visiting in Italy the beautiful sanctuary of Saint Mary of Canneto. Can you imagine that the solar panels covering the roof of the site for outdoor worship produce enough energy for the whole sanctuary? That's a practical example to follow.

During the last century, the Elder Amphilochios Makris of Patmos (1889–1970), recently canonized by the Ecumenical Patriarchate, often gave as a penance to the people coming to confess to him to plant a tree. Over the years, the arid island of Saint John the Evangelist became a green island. The Elder used to say: "Who plants a tree plants hope, plants peace, plants love, and receives the blessings of God." He considered that there was another commandment of God, not written in the Scriptures: "Love the trees." May the Holy Elder Amphilochios encourage us to move from eco-theology towards eco-justice, and to implement orthodoxy by orthopraxis, by planting trees as a sign of our conversion.

FINAL STATEMENT

We, the participants at the Fifth Halki Summit entitled "Sustaining the Future of the Planet Together"—an international and interdisciplinary conference co-organized by the Ecumenical Patriarchate and the Sophia University Institute, inspired by the prophetic magisterium of Patriarch Bartholomew and Pope Francis—wish to appeal to our churches and to all those who care about our common home:

The sincere communication and mutual attentiveness, as well as the open exchange of ecclesial approaches and reflections experienced throughout our summit (June 8–11, 2022), have led us to discover that we are at a decisive turning point for the future of the human family, in which our churches are called to play an essential educational role through the "Global Compact on Education."

The challenge or opportunity to which we are called is that of developing a shared ecological ethos. As artisans of peace and fraternity, we seek to implement good practices, committing ourselves to work on interdisciplinary pathways for the formation of new paradigms that can interpret and transform reality. In this way, we aspire to overcome the culture of waste, knowing that what we do to our world "we also do to the least of our brothers and sisters" (Matt 25:40).

Therefore, with conviction and gratitude we embrace the exhortation of Ecumenical Patriarch Bartholomew: "Always remember that our vocation as Christians is about making and reinforcing connections between ourselves and all of God's creation, between our faith and our action, between our theology and our spirituality, between what we say and what we do, between science and religion, between our beliefs and every discipline, between our sacramental communion and our social consciousness, between our generation and the generations to come, just as between heaven and earth, between our two churches, but also with other churches and other faith communities."

https://www.halkisummit.com/hs5/participants/

BIOGRAPHICAL NOTES

EDITORS

John Chryssavgis is Archdeacon of the Ecumenical Patriarchate, Executive Director of the Huffington Ecumenical Institute, and Professor of Theology at Holy Cross School of Theology. His books include *Dialogue of Love* (Fordham University Press, 2014) and *Theology, Ecology, and Ecumenism* (Washington Theological Consortium, 2023).

Angela Caliaro graduated as a business correspondent in foreign languages. She lived with the Focolare in Istanbul (2006–2019), dedicating her time to ecumenism and interreligious dialogue. Currently she is Secretary of the "Patriarch Athenagoras-Chiara Lubich" Ecumenical Chair of Sophia University Institute in Loppiano (Florence, Italy).

CONTRIBUTORS

Giuseppe Argiolas is Stable Extraordinary Professor of Management at Sophia University Institute. His publications include *Social Management: Principles, Governance and Practice* (Springer, 2017).

Nikolaos Asproulis is currently deputy director of the Volos Academy for Theological Studies and lecturer at the Hellenic Open University. His latest publication includes (co-edited with John Chryssavgis) *Priests of Creation: John Zizioulas on Discerning an Ecological Ethos* (T&T Clark: London-New York, 2021).

Augustinos Bairactaris is Associate Professor at the Ecclesiastical Academy of Heraklion, Crete. He studied theology at the Universities of Thessaloniki, Fribourg, and Geneva. The author of many articles on theology, ecumenism, and ecology, his latest book is *Jesus Forsaken and the Spirituality of the Focolare Movement* (Epikentro, 2021).

Vincenzo Buonomo is Full Professor of International Law at the Pontifical Lateran University (Vatican City). He has served as President of the Pontifical Lateran University (2018–2022) and Advisor to the Pontifical Councils for Inter-Religious Dialogue and for Legislative Texts. He is the author of publications on international law and environmental law.

Msgr. Piero Coda is Secretary General of the International Theological Commission and Member of the Joint International Commission for Theological Dialogue between the Catholic Church and the Orthodox Church. He was the first President of Sophia University Institute (2008–2020), where he is Professor of Trinitarian Ontology. His books include *From the Trinity: The Coming of God in Theology and Revelation* (Catholic University of America, 2020).

Chris Durante is Associate Professor of Theology at Saint Peter's University (USA). His academic interests are in religion, ethics, science, and society, including ecological theology and environmental ethics. His essays are found in many journals, including at: https://publicorthodoxy.org/author/chris-durante/.

Metropolitan Job of Pisidia is the Orthodox bishop of the region of Antalya, Turkey. He is the co-president of the Joint International Commission for the Theological Dialogue between the Roman Catholic Church and the Orthodox Church. He teaches liturgy at the Catholic University of Paris.

Margaret Karram was born in Haifa, holds a BA in Jewish Studies from the American Jewish University (Los Angeles), and is current President of the Focolare Movement. She received the Mount Zion Award for Reconciliation (2013) and the Saint Rita International Prize for promoting interfaith dialogue (2016). Her publications include *Per non sfiorarci invano* (Edizioni Francescane Italiane, 2023).

Vasilios N. Makrides has been since 1999 Professor for Religious Studies (specializing in Orthodox Christianity) at the Faculty of Philosophy of the University of Erfurt, Germany. He recently coedited *Orthodoxy in the Agora: Orthodox Christian Political Theologies across History* (Vandenhoeck & Ruprecht, 2024).

Sandra Ferreira Ribeiro studied physics and sociology of religion, earning a doctorate at Sophia University with a thesis entitled *The Meeting of Patriarch Athenagoras and Chiara Lubich: Between History and Prophecy* (forthcoming). She co-directs the Center "One" for Christian Unity, the ecumenical secretariat of the Focolare Movement.

Sergio Rondinara is Professor of Epistemology at Sophia University Institute. He graduated in Nuclear Engineering from the Sapienza University of Rome and obtained a licentiate in Philosophy of Nature and Fundamental Theology from the Pontifical Gregorian University. Among his publications is *Interpretazione del reale fra scienze e teologia* (Città Nuova, 2007).

Msgr. Angelo Vincenzo Zani studied philosophy and theology at the Brescia Seminary, the Angelicum, and the Lateran University, where he received a doctorate in theology. He worked in the Congregation for Catholic Education from 2002, serving as Secretary (2012–2022). He is currently the Archivist and Librarian of the Holy Roman Church.

FURTHER READING

ECUMENICAL PATRIARCH BARTHOLOMEW

- Ecumenical Patriarch Bartholomew, *On Earth As in Heaven*, edited by John Chryssavgis (Bronx, NY: Fordham University Press, 2011)
- Ecumenical Patriarch Bartholomew, *Encountering the Mystery: Understanding Orthodox Christianity Today* (New York: Doubleday, 2008)

POPE FRANCIS

- Pope Francis, *Laudato Si': On Care for Our Common Home* (Huntington, IN: Our Sunday Visitor, 2015)
  » For the original Latin, see: https://www.vatican.va/content/francesco/la/encyclicals/documents/papa-francesco_20150524_enciclica-laudato-si.html

- » For the official English translation, see: https://www.vatican.va/content/francesco/en/encyclicals/documents/papa-francesco_20150524_enciclica-laudato-si.html
- Pope Francis, *Fratelli Tutti: On Fraternity and Social Friendship* (Huntington, IN: Our Sunday Visitor, 2020)
  - » For the Latin, see: https://www.vatican.va/content/francesco/la/encyclicals/documents/papa-francesco_20201003_enciclica-fratelli-tutti.html
  - » For the official English translation, see: https://www.vatican.va/content/francesco/en/encyclicals/documents/papa-francesco_20201003_enciclica-fratelli-tutti.html

OTHER SOURCES

- Chiara Lubich, *Essential Writings: Spirituality, Dialogue, Culture* (Hyde Park, NY: New City Press, 2007)
- Official texts of the Holy and Great Council of the Orthodox Church in English, see: https://www.holycouncil.org/
- Ecumenical Patriarchate, *For the Life of the World: The Social Ethos of the Orthodox Church*, edited by David Bentley Hart and John Chryssavgis (Brookline, MA: Holy Cross Orthodox Press, 2020)

www.ingramcontent.com/pod-product-compliance
Lightning Source LLC
Chambersburg PA
CBHW050929240426